D0857414

North Riverside Public Library
2400 S. Des Plaines Ave.
North Riverside, IL 60546
708-447-0869
www.northriversidelibrary.org

Casey & the Flying Fortress

The True Story of a World War II Bomber Pilot and the Crew.

To The PATRONS OF The
North Riverside LIBRARY,

I hope You Enjoy Reading my Book!

Mark Farina

authorHOUSE®

AuthorHouse™
1663 Liberty Drive
Bloomington, IN 47403
www.authorhouse.com
Phone: 1 (800) 839-8640

Published by AuthorHouse   10/17/2016

ISBN: 978-1-5246-3833-7 (sc)
ISBN: 978-1-5246-3834-4 (hc)
ISBN: 978-1-5246-3832-0 (e)

Library of Congress Control Number: 2016914808

Print information available on the last page.

This book is printed on acid-free paper.

Contents

Foreword
By
Diane Paulinski Farina, CASEY'S Middle Daughter

It is with mixed emotions that I received all the information that has come to pass from my husband Mark's research on my Father Casey and his B-17 Bomber crew.

With each new discovery I shared Mark's excitement, fascination and pride. This included receiving letters, pictures, phone conversations and on some occasions, meeting crew members or their wives. I was especially elated to receive letters and emails from the Netherlands from the family who sheltered my dad and two fellow crew members. It brought a tear to my eyes when I actually spoke on the phone with Pietertje from the Netherlands. She was only 16 years old when her family as part of the Dutch Underground, sheltered my dad and crew. Despite the language difference, I got to tell her "Thank You" and we both said "I Love You" to each other.

Mark and I shared new discoveries with my sisters Nini and Linda, but all the while I couldn't help but feel sad and melancholy that my mom, Lennie and brother, Jamie were not here to share in the excitement of finding out how well liked and respected my Dad was by the crew.

Jamie was so proud of his Daddy, we all were. I can remember as far back as the early 60's when my Dad said to us "If anyone ever asks you, you can tell them that I was a Captain in the Air Force. I want you to be proud of me."

We Are Proud of You, Daddy.

Love, Diane

P.S. You can be proud of your Grandson, Louis. He helped me proofread this book of Mark's with just as much enthusiasm. I am also very proud of my Husband Mark for his persistence, enthusiasm and the countless hours of research and writing this book.

Thank you to my Aunt Joanne Paulinski Dryjan for lovingly transcribing my Dad's World War II recollections "From Heaven In To Hell", creating a World War II Scrapbook for my Dad, and being the dedicated family historian.

A Letter From Louis Farina (Casey's Grandson)

Dear Papa Casey,

All my life I have heard about you and how brave you were in World War II, and now this book my Dad is writing about you. Now that I am 17 years old, how I wish I could meet you and Uncle Jamie.

I have heard so much about what a good Daddy you were to my Mom, Diane, my Aunts Nini and Linda, and my Uncle Jamie and Husband to Grammie. How you loved swimming in the backyard pool with them at night, with the spotlight on. At backyard pool parties, how you and Grammie sold hot dogs and potato chips for a penny at your pretend grocery store, and had all the neighborhood kids call you Uncle Casey.

If I had you here with me now, I would tell you all about all my favorite classic rock bands and maybe take you to a few concerts.

How I wish,...
Your Loving Grandson, Louis

I Dedicate this to My Loving Wife, Diane and Our Son, Louis who have been my inspiration on this journey of discovery that lead to the writing of this book. To My Father-in-Law Casey Paulinski whom I never met but have gotten to know more about and grown to admire for his courage both during World War II and in his health challenges after the war. My Mother-in-Law Lennie Paulinski for her incredible love and generosity and being able to keep her family together during the most difficult circumstances, and to my Parents, Rose & Louis Farina, whose dynamic personalities have always been my inspiration.

Introduction

Casimir "Casey" Paulinski was the father-in-law I never met. He died after an arduous nine-year battle with cancer in 1974, many years before I met my wife, Diane. I knew that Casey was an Army Air Corps veteran who had been the copilot of a B-17 bomber during World War II, that his plane had been shot down, and that he had been a prisoner of war in Germany.

I also knew that while he was a POW, Casey had helped dig tunnels to try to escape the camps and that during the worst of the internment, toward the end of the war, he and other prisoners had survived starvation by eating things that would make most people cringe.

After the war, he worked for the Ford Motor Company at an aircraft engine manufacturing plant on Chicago's southwest side, testing jet engines. The site would become Ford City Shopping Center. Later, Casey was a bus driver for the Chicago Transit Authority.

Aside from these basic facts shared by my wife and my mother-in-law, Leanore "Lennie" Paulinski, I knew only about his struggles with cancer and about his untimely death at the relatively young age of fifty-four.

Of the few photos of my father-in-law that I had seen, the most notable was of him and his crew posing in front of a B-17 during the war. His wife and three daughters all had framed copies of this photo, which hangs in a hallway in our home along with other family photos.

Casey did not talk much about his war experiences with his children, so my wife had few details to share with me. I imagine that it was awfully difficult for this man to endure all that he did with his illness and that he was not in a hurry to reminisce about a period that may have contributed to his failing health.

I would begin to learn much more about Casey in September of 2001, and what I discovered would have a profound effect not only on me but on my wife and her family and the living members of his bomber crew.

The experiences I will share in this book have given me an even better appreciation of the sacrifices these veterans made for our country and of the sacrifices all who have served in the armed forces make.

I have always admired veterans. My father, Louis Farina, an army veteran of World War II, received the Purple Heart and the Bronze Star Medal for Gallantry for his service with the medical corps in Europe, which included the Battle of the Bulge. His experiences in the war and during the rest of his life probably warrant their own book.

My maternal grandfather, James Torina, served in the US Army in World War I, although he didn't see combat while in France. My uncle, Joe Farina, served stateside during World War II in the Army Air Corps, and another uncle, Vito Torina, was stationed in Germany with the army during the Korean War. Our family suffered tragedy when my mom's cousin, Pvt. Nicholas Castronova, was killed while serving with the army during the Battle of the Bulge in France. He was only eighteen.

My search for information about my father-in-law was unlike any other experience in my life. This project became almost a mission. I was quite focused, and the results were extraordinarily gratifying. The discovery of new information, particularly from firsthand accounts, left me feeling almost euphoric.

All of this came about through a combination of luck, fate, hard work, and something close to divine intervention. I made numerous telephone calls, spent hours on the Internet, traveled to both coasts of the United States and to Europe, and researched many books and other publications about the US Army Air Forces in World War II.

In this book I will tell the story of Casey Paulinski, a young man from the South Side of Chicago who became a soldier, a bomber pilot, and a POW. I will share the memories of relatives, crewmates, and a member of a family in the Netherlands that sheltered Casey and two crewmates after they had been shot down. I will also offer material from other sources, some previously published, some discovered on historical websites and in other places.

While the stories of the airmen of World War II are well documented, each man has a unique identity that makes telling and retelling these stories important. It would be the ultimate disrespect to forget the heroism and the sacrifice of these men. Because of them, Americans have been able to live in relative peace, comfort, and above all freedom.

This book will also tell the remarkable story of how sixty years later, either through sheer luck or by fate, we were able to find the people who were there during World War II and who could tell this story and answer the questions so often asked since the end of the war. My only regret is that Casey and Lennie were not here to share these discoveries.

Special thanks go to the crew members and their families, who provided valuable information, insight, and inspiration for this book—in particular, pilot Hank Roeber and wife, Ruth, who graciously hosted Diane, Louis, and me at their home in southern Illinois. Radio operator Hubert O'Neil and his wife Betty also shared their memories, graciously welcomed us into their home for an overnight stay, and took us around Cape Cod. Bombardier George Sokolsky and waist gunner Royce McGillvary took the time to meet with me in Los Angeles and to share their memories.

Josephine Sybo, wife of flight engineer and top turret gunner Walt Sybo, and their daughter Sharyn Ashburn shared valuable information, as did Blanche Sumpter, wife of tail gunner Irvin Sumpter. Lillian Verlo, wife of ball turret gunner Clayton Verlo, and their daughter Karen made a copy of an audiotape of Clayton's war memories, particularly about his time spent as a POW at Stalag 17B. Patricia Townsend Pratt, niece of navigator Donald McPhee, shared photos from the POW camp and helped solve a Decades old mystery surrounding the whereabouts of some crew members. Arthur Pinzke, a B-17 copilot from Chicago who trained with Casey and was in the same squadron and POW camp, shared his memories and was a source of inspiration.

Finally, I am most grateful to our friends in the Netherlands, Til Kenkhuis and Pietertje Pieters.

Chapter 1

Fate Takes Us on a Journey

Our journey of discovery began in late September of 2001 when my wife, Diane, and I were planning to take my mother-in-law, Lennie, for lunch at a new restaurant at Chicago's North Avenue Beach on Lake Michigan.

We had called the day before to make sure the restaurant was still open for the season, which was to close the following day. As soon as we arrived at the lakefront, we discovered that a special event was taking place and that we would have to park a few blocks away. Because my wife and my mother-in-law had limited mobility, we instead decided to go to the popular Navy Pier with its restaurants, shops, and other attractions.

I mentioned that divine intervention seemed to play a part in this story. It began on this day because as soon as we reached the Navy Pier, we discovered that the parking lot was virtually full. We changed plans entirely and decided to drive in the opposite direction and go to a favorite restaurant of ours in the northwest suburb of Wheeling, a twenty-eight-mile journey.

After lunch at Bob Chinn's Crab House, we made our way back toward Westchester, where my mother-in-law lived. We drove by Palwaukee Airport (now called Chicago Executive Airport) and immediately noticed what looked like a vintage World War II aircraft parked on the tarmac next to one of the airplane hangars along Milwaukee Avenue. The plane had attracted a crowd of people.

Diane asked me to call the airport on the cell phone to get more information. The aircraft, a B-17 from World War II, was touring the country with a stop in the Chicago area. Diane then asked me to turn around and go back to the airport so we could see the type of airplane her father had flown. As we headed back, it suddenly occurred to Diane that it was her father's birthday, September 21st and Lennie said that she had never seen a B-17 up close.

It was like some unseen force had steered us in the direction of that airplane, from lakefront Chicago to Wheeling.

As we approached Palwaukee Airport, suddenly there it was, shining in the bright afternoon sun, the silver-colored B-17 named *Sentimental Journey*, with its famous artwork of actress and pin-up girl Betty Grable. Fortunately there wasn't a huge crowd, and we were able to go right up to the aircraft.

After securing tickets, I climbed aboard the plane and quickly discovered how cramped and claustrophobic it was inside. Men had to be young, thin, and healthy to pull themselves into the cockpit area (they didn't typically use a ladder) or to squeeze into the cramped space for the tail gunner or the ball turret gunner.

Considering that they were in these tight quarters for eight to ten hours, mostly in subzero conditions, wearing parachute harnesses and other heavy equipment and clothing, I could appreciate the creature comforts of airline travel today. Having been inside, I could only imagine what it must have been like for the men as they were bombarded by German antiaircraft flak and shot at by enemy fighter planes, all the while staying in tight formation as they approached their targets.

Diane, Louis, and Lennie viewed the plane from the outside and talked to a crew member, a World War II veteran who had flown B-17s. We took a few photos of the plane and of ourselves with the aircraft in the background. Lennie was restricted to a portable wheelchair, but we took her to the rear entrance, which was at ground level. She stood up, climbed the short stepladder, and peered into the back of the aircraft that her husband Casey had flown fifty-eight years earlier.

After a few more glances at the aircraft, we made our way back home, all the while talking about our good fortune in seeing the Flying Fortress.

On October 9, we celebrated Diane's birthday at Lennie's condo in Westchester about twenty miles west of downtown Chicago. Lennie had ordered a green-dinosaur Halloween costume for Louis that she was looking forward to seeing him wear. Our two-and-a-half-year-old son put on this adorable costume with its long tail and pranced around the living room to the delight of Lennie and everyone else.

This was the last time we would see Lennie alive. Just two days later, Diane's sister Nini discovered that she had died while sitting in her recliner, probably watching the news about 9/11 on television. And to think, only a few weeks earlier, something had brought us on an unexpected journey to see an old military airplane that Lennie's husband had flown in World War II.

If the story ended there, it would be interesting enough, but this was only the beginning of a historical journey that would take Diane and me from Chicago to St. Louis and on to Cape Cod, Massachusetts, and eventually bring me to Los Angeles and all the way to the Netherlands. We also ventured on the information superhighway (the Internet) and got on the telephone to communicate with key people in that country.

Facing the death of one parent is difficult enough, but Diane and her two sisters now had to confront the reality that both of their parents were gone. They also had to deal with settling Lennie's estate and selling her condo. All the while we were also trying to sell our home near Midway Airport and were living in the basement of my parents' house in the Galewood neighborhood of Chicago while our house was on the market.

It was eerie to return to Lennie's condo to look through personal papers, clothes, and all the other items that make up a home and a life. Each day brought a new discovery and many times a tear to our eyes.

This was a new experience for me. I had never lost a loved one so close, other than a grandparent. I also had to help make the funeral arrangements and to share the emotional toll Lennie's death had on my wife.

Lennie was a wonderful mother-in-law and a good friend to all who were lucky enough to have come in contact with her. She was extremely generous, and in the nine years that I knew her, she never had an angry or negative thing to say to me. She also had an endearing way of expressing surprise and enthusiasm about even the simplest of life's occurrences.

I discovered that my mother-in-law had saved many photos and had assembled them in scrapbooks. We found old photos of Diane, of her sisters Nini and Linda, and of their beloved brother, Jamie, who tragically died in an auto accident at age nineteen while visiting his sister in Kansas. Jamie had planned to follow in his father's military footsteps, having recently enlisted in the US Marine Corps, and was looking forward to basic training. There were also photos of Lennie and Casey as a young couple after World War II and pictures of the family in happier times.

One day as we were rummaging through all of Lennie's belongings, we stumbled upon a scrapbook about Casey from World War II. Its faded pages contained a treasure trove of information. There were photos of Casey in basic training, first with the army infantry at Fort Bragg in North Carolina and later in pilot training at Victory Field in Vernon, Texas.

This remarkable collection helped tell the story of how Casey, like so many other young American men, had enlisted in the armed forces shortly after the Japanese bombing of Pearl Harbor on December 7, 1941. There were postcards from Casey to his mother and father and later the dreaded Western Union telegrams informing his family that he was missing in action and then confirmed as a POW of the Germans.

Casey's sister Joanne, who had compiled a similar scrapbook for her husband Ed Dryjan while he was in the service, had lovingly assembled this one. Most telling were the short letters from Casey while he was a POW at Stalag Luft 1 in Barth, Germany. For the first time, we learned that his plane had been shot down on December 22, 1943. We would later discover that the German SS had captured Casey and two other crew members three days later on Christmas Day.

The scrapbook also contained the joyous telegram informing Casey's family that he was under Allied control when the camp was liberated in March 1945, fourteen months later.

Paging through the scrapbook was like taking a trip back in time—not to peek at some vague historical figure we had read about in history books or had seen on a television documentary but to follow someone who was not only real for us but who was the father Diane dearly loved and had lost at the age of sixteen.

I was interested in learning more about Casey and what had happened to him and the crew. However, I didn't give the subject much more thought until we had closed on the sale of our house in December and until after the Christmas and New Year's holidays, which were difficult and somber with the recent loss of Diane's mom. I had no magic plan to find out more details about Casey and the crew. The project seemed to happen by accident and to develop a life of its own.

Chapter 2

The Air War in Europe

With the surprise attack on the United States Pacific Fleet at Pearl Harbor on December 7, 1941, America was officially thrust into World War II. The full impact of American involvement in the war, particularly in Europe and North Africa, would come over time as America and the Allied forces developed their industrial and military capacity and transported supplies, equipment, and men to England and North Africa.

The British had been courageously fighting the German Luftwaffe virtually alone since the beginning of the war. Royal Air Force (RAF) fighters defended their homeland in the Battle of Britain during the summer of 1940. Then the British faced the onslaught of the Germans during the devastating blitz of London and other cities. The heroism and the determination of the British in withstanding German attacks cannot be exaggerated. If not for Britain's efforts, the American Army Air Forces would never have been able to create bases in England and, in combination with RAF bombers such as the Avro Lancaster and the Vickers-Armstrong Wellington, to eventually claim air supremacy over Europe.

More than sixteen million young American men and women enlisted or were drafted into the armed forces and began training in the marines, the army, the air forces, the navy, the coast guard, and the merchant marine.

The United States Air Forces were then a part of the army known as the Army Air Corps. Not until after the war would they become a separate branch, the US Air Force.

The bomber crews came from many backgrounds, from the East Coast and the West, from the North and the South, from the big city, farms, and small towns. These widely diverse individuals trained together stateside and became one unit before making the perilous journey across the Atlantic Ocean by troop ship.

One thing most of them had in common was that they were young kids suddenly asked to grow up quickly so that they could save the world from the oppression of Nazi Germany, fascist Italy, and imperialist Japan.

In Europe and North Africa, the Army Air Corps consisted of the Eighth, Ninth, Twelfth, and Fifteenth Air Forces. The Ninth was originally based in Egypt and participated in Allied operations across much of North Africa before moving to England. The Twelfth operated in the Mediterranean Theater out of North Africa, and the Fifteenth operated from bases in Italy after the Allied forces secured Sicily and most of the mainland.

The most famous of the air forces serving in this theater of the war was the mighty Eighth Air Force, based in England. Casey Paulinski and the crew of his B-17 Flying Fortress would meet their destiny as part of the Eighth Air Force's Ninety-Second Bomb Group, 407th Bomb Squadron, based in Podington, England.

While the Boeing B-17 Flying Fortress was the most celebrated and publicized of the heavy and medium bombers in World War II, it was by no means the most mass produced or the most used heavy bomber. The Consolidated B-24 Liberator and its crews played an equally significant role in winning the air war in Europe. In addition, the twin-engine North American B-25 Mitchell bombers and the Martin B-26 Marauder made important contributions to the success of the American and Allied efforts.

For more than sixty years the crews of the B-17s and the B-24s, airplane buffs, and historians have debated the virtues of the planes. While there is no clear-cut verdict as to which was better, the spirited debates will continue as long as there is a fascination with historical aircraft.

The B-17 and the B-24 were four-engine heavy bombers, which saw the lion's share of missions over Europe. Both aircraft were designed for ten-man crews: a pilot and a copilot, a bombardier, a navigator, a flight engineer/top turret gunner, a radio operator, a ball turret gunner, two waist gunners (left and right), and a tail gunner. As the war progressed, B-24 crews were trimmed to nine men.

Though the air corps may have seemed exciting and even glamorous to those trying to join or to people back home reading about its exploits, the bombing missions were extraordinarily dangerous and emotionally challenging for the brave men who ventured skyward.

I was surprised to learn that the bomber crews in England suffered more casualties than the marines fighting the bloody battles in the South Pacific. Early in the war, the Army Air Corps said a bomber crew carrying out twenty-five missions had completed its tour of duty and could return home, but it was statistically impossible for a crew to survive that many missions. The casualty rate was that high.

Aircrews had advantages on the ground: reasonably comfortable beds, usually in barracks, hot meals, and entertainment at local pubs or while on leave in the big city, London. This was heaven compared with what the combat soldier endured: sleeping outdoors in all kinds of weather, scrounging for food, or eating K-rations from a can.

The airmen forgot all these advantages as soon as their planes took off on a mission and they struggled to get into and stay in formation on the way to the target and to fend off German antiaircraft artillery flak and enemy fighter planes.

These were the circumstances that Casey Paulinski, Hank Roeber, and the crew of their B-17 Flying Fortress faced as they set off on a mission to Osnabruck, Germany, to bomb railroad marshalling yards on December 22, 1943. On this fateful day, as they made their fifth mission together, there would be a new man aboard the B-17.

Staff Sgt. Royce McGillvary, a native of Gary, Indiana, who had grown up in Nova Scotia, Canada, replaced waist gunner Lawrence Anderson, a Boston native who had been killed in an accident on the ground in Podington. McGillvary took Anderson's spot alongside Sy Wolfson. McGillvary had been a replacement on a number of missions with different crews but was never assigned to a permanent one. Hubert O'Neill had been sidelined for three of the previous missions due to a severely infected toe, which had kept him hospitalized.

In the front of the B-17 were the officers, typically second lieutenants: bombardier George Sokolsky of Rochester, New York; navigator Donald

McPhee of Burlingame, California; pilot Hank Roeber of Long Island, New York, and copilot Casimir "Casey" Paulinski of Chicago, Illinois. Directly behind these officers were enlisted men, all staff sergeants: the flight engineer and top turret gunner, Walter Sybo of Pittsburgh, Pennsylvania; radio operator Hubert O'Neill of Lynn, Massachusetts; ball turret gunner Clayton Verlo of LaCrosse, Wisconsin; waist gunners Seymour "Sy" Wolfson of Akron, Ohio, Royce McGillvary originally from Gary, Indiana, and tail gunner Irvin Sumpter of Ramona, Oklahoma.

The crew had assembled and had begun training on the B-17 at Moses Lake and in Spokane, Washington, in the summer of 1943.

Chapter 3

Casimir Jerome Paulinski

Casimir Jerome "Casey" Paulinski was born on September 21, 1919, in Chicago, Illinois. He was the youngest of three children born to Adam and Eleanor Paulinski, immigrants from Poland. Casey grew up in the Brighton Park neighborhood on Chicago's southwest side and attended Tilden Technical High School. Before enlisting in the military, he worked as a printing pressman at the Coyner Company.

Casey's first cousin, Joe Bruch, remembered him as being a fun-loving, likable guy whom he palled around with in their youth. Bruch would serve in the navy as a torpedo man second class in the Philippines, New Guinea, and other spots in the South Pacific during the war.

Like millions of other young American men, Casey enlisted in the military for the required year of service. On April 3, 1941, he was inducted into the army at Camp Grant in Rockford, Illinois. After three days and two nights of travel by train, he arrived at Fort Bragg, North Carolina, for basic training and was assigned to Battery B, Fourteenth Battalion, Fifth Training Regiment, Field Artillery Replacement Center.

His first two weeks were spent quarantined with other new recruits to safeguard against any disease or illness that could be spread to other soldiers.

Loneliness and the rigors of basic training took their toll. Casey wrote to his parents on April 12 that one soldier had committed suicide and another had gone on a four-day hunger strike. In general, life as a private in basic training was monotonous.

Social activities on the base were limited, so Casey spent much of his free time writing letters home to his parents and his sister Joanne. In his letters, he often asked about his young niece Virgie, daughter of Joanne and husband Ed, and about his nephew Dennis, son of his brother Dan and wife Bea.

Training consisted of everything from learning to drive a truck to small- arms and machine-gun practice. Casey seemed to welcome the strict discipline and the routine, but like any soldier, he yearned for a three-day pass so he could return home.

Casey received a plum assignment when he was assigned as a driver for a colonel. This meant getting up extra early to open the colonel's office at 6:30 a.m., but Casey got to see the brass up close and to break the monotony of other responsibilities. During his time at Fort Bragg, he also traveled through much of North and South Carolina and remarked that the people in the small towns and cities away from camp were much friendlier than the townsfolk near the army base. He particularly enjoyed the sixty-mile trip to North Carolina's capital, Raleigh.

One of Casey's favorite leisure activities was to see the latest movies including *Strawberry Blonde*, starring James Cagney, Olivia de Havilland, and Rita Hayworth, and the Abbott-and-Costello comedy *In the Navy*, co-starring Dick Powell and the Andrews Sisters.

After four months Casey and his battalion were transferred to the Indiantown Gap Military Reservation near Pennsylvania's capital, Harrisburg. Here Casey received his first furlough home. During maneuvers with his regiment, he got a taste of the South, traveling through cities like Richmond and Fredericksburg, Virginia; Macon, Georgia, and Vicksburg, Mississippi.

By 1942 he had made his way to Louisiana and to military camps in Beauregard and Livingston. At Camp Livingston during the summer of 1942, he applied for and was accepted in the Army Air Forces.

In a congratulatory letter to Casey's parents, Maj. Gen. H. R. Harmon, the commanding officer of the Army Air Forces Classification School in San Antonio, Texas, wrote, "The duties of an Army Pilot call for a high degree of mental and physical alertness, sound judgment and an inherent aptitude for flying. Men who make good material for flying as pilots are rare. The Classification Board believes that your boy is one of them."

It was a proud moment for the family. The Paulinski's baby boy was going to be a pilot with the United States Army Air Forces.

Pilot training

The first stops for Casey Paulinski on his journey to earning his wings and becoming a pilot were the Army Air Force Classification Center and the preflight school at Randolph Field in San Antonio, Texas. Here challenging testing and training gave him a taste of what lay ahead. A new training tool for Casey's class of 43-G was the high-altitude pressure chamber, which gave the cadets a sense of how their bodies would react to being in an unpressurized aircraft at twenty-five thousand feet.

In this setting and later in primary training at Victory Field in Vernon, Texas, many young men would drop out or wash out and be reassigned to train in areas such as navigator, radio operator, bombardier, and gunnery school. At Victory Field, Casey met Arthur Pinzke, a fellow Chicagoan who was also a pilot cadet.

Casey and Art's air corps experiences would remain intertwined throughout the rest of war. Not only did they train together at Victory Field and in Oklahoma, but they were also assigned as B-17 copilots at Moses Lake and in Spokane, Washington, and placed in the same squadron in England, the 407th.

They would also be shot down three months apart and spend the rest of the war in the same POW camp, Stalag Luft 1, although in separate compounds.

Art Pinzke

Art Pinzke was born on May 20, 1916, in Chicago and grew up in the heavily German-American Lincoln Square neighborhood on the North Side. He attended Theodore Roosevelt High School before transferring to and graduating from Amundsen High School. He was the only member of his family to finish high school, his two half-brothers having gone to work during the Great Depression to help the family survive.

His father, Arthur Pinzke, had emigrated from Germany, and his mother had been born in Chicago. His mother was widowed with two boys when she remarried and gave birth to Arthur just before America's entry into World War I. After high school, Art, with a helping hand from his two brothers, worked as a pressman for the Chicago Law Printing Company.

Like Casey, Art originally enlisted in the army infantry before applying for and being accepted by the air corps. Art described air cadet training as "exciting and challenging." "We all loved it," he said about learning to fly. "It was also better than having to stay in the infantry."

During their five months of preflight training in San Antonio, Texas, cadets spent most of their time in the classroom, learning about the theory of flying, the mechanical elements, and other details about aeronautics. They also took courses in physics, current events, geography, and civil air regulations. In total they received seven hundred hours of academic and military training. They also participated in training on how to cope with a lack of oxygen.

"They would put five or six of us in this chamber and ask us to write our names without any oxygen," said Art. "We would all pass out while writing. Then they would pump oxygen into the chamber, and we would suddenly come to and continue writing our names and not even know that we had passed out. It taught us the importance of keeping your oxygen mask on above a certain altitude."

Physical endurance was also vital for any pilot, so the cadets participated in many long cross-country runs and other strenuous challenges.

In primary training at Victory Field in Vernon, Texas, cadets got their first taste of flying, heading up in open-air, single-engine BT-19 planes with an instructor.

"The first time up many of us wondered what we were getting ourselves into," said Art, "but after the required eight hours of training with an instructor we looked forward to going solo."

The most frightening aspect of flight training for cadets was the first time they were asked to make a nighttime landing. "We went up at dusk," Art said, "and after flying around for a little while, it was now completely dark, so it was a bit scary to have to find the runway lights and guide that aircraft down to a safe landing."

Not everyone accepted as a cadet was able to earn his wings. Many a young man washed out voluntarily or for a variety of reasons including accidents and other mistakes.

In basic training at Enid Army Air Field in Oklahoma, cadets flew on BT-15s, twin-engine Cessnas. "These planes could carry four people, and our training flights were longer and more complicated," Art said. "We would have to practice navigational techniques and how to fly a plane using instrumentation rather than by touch."

As the cadets spent more time in the air, they developed a growing confidence in their ability to handle an aircraft, and they looked forward with excitement to earning their wings and becoming fighter pilots.

Accidents during training, while not frequent, did happen, and Art recalled that in at least one instance, a cadet lost his life. But the thrill of flying helped the cadets overcome any fear. The final stop for Casey and Art was Frederick Army Air Field in Oklahoma where they received advanced training and finally got their coveted wings. There they trained on twin-engine bombers—B-25s and B-26s.

Casey would learn that he would be assigned to a B-17 Bomber crew lead by a 2nd Lieutenant Henry Roeber and train on the four engine aircraft in the State of Washington

Assigned To A Crew

Hank Roeber

Henry "Hank" Roeber was born on August 26, 1919, in Brooklyn, New York. He was the only child of Harry and Ursula Roeber and grew up on Long Island in Queens County. He graduated from Richmond Hill High School in 1937.

Hank came from a family of railroad men and eventually worked for the Pennsylvania Railroad in a dining car. He was drafted into the army, and like Casey Paulinski, Art Pinzke, and so many others, he took a chance and applied for pilot training in the Army Air Forces.

He received his primary training at Thompson-Robbins Field in West Helena, Arkansas, and recalled his first experience in the air as "scary and enough of this!"

After overcoming his initial fears, Hank continued on the path toward earning his wings, undergoing basic training at Gunter Field in Montgomery, Alabama, and then advanced training at Columbus Army Air Field in Mississippi where he graduated with the class of 43-D.

"I really wanted to be assigned to tactical aircraft like A-20s and B-26s, but I was certainly very proud to be the pilot and chief of a B-17 crew helping defend our country," said Hank.

Hank had other important considerations on his mind during pilot training. He and Ruth Smith were married in 1942.

Hank and the rest of the B-17 crew would come together at Geiger Field in Spokane, Washington.

Hubert O'Neill

Hubert O'Neill was born on October 8, 1924, in Lynn, Massachusetts. He was the sixth of seven children born to Lester and Catherine O'Neil. After turning eighteen and graduating from Lynn English High School in 1942, Hubert enlisted in the Army Air Corps. His training as a radio operator took him to places such as Florida; Sioux Falls, South Dakota, and eventually Washington state where he became part of a B-17 crew.

George Sokolsky

George Sokolsky had initially hoped to be a pilot, but he had trouble with the aerobatics portion of primary training, and after six hours in the air with an instructor, he washed out. He was then transferred to bombardier and navigation training.

"I had no regrets washing out," said George. "It worked out okay because I could have wound up like a couple of my fellow cadets, who were killed in a midair collision while in training." George, who was married, had the grim responsibility of telling the wife of one of the pilots that her husband had been killed. "My wife, Evelyn, was rooming with this pilot's wife, so they asked me to tell her the terrible news."

George was born October 16, 1916, in Auburn, New York. He was the second oldest of seven children born to Myron and Mary Sokolsky. His father, born in Ukraine, worked at Ukrainian churches, directing the choirs and teaching Ukrainian school. This led the family to move frequently during George's childhood. He spent most of his youth in Pennsylvania, living in Wilkes-Barre and Hanover among other places. He graduated from Nanticoke High School in 1934 and shortly thereafter moved with this family to Rochester, New York.

He originally received a deferment from the military draft because he was the oldest sibling at home, taking care of his mother, who had suffered a stroke and was confined to a wheelchair. His father's church duties kept him away from home.

After his father returned home to stay, George enlisted in the Army Air Corps in 1942. He was assigned to preflight school across the country in Santa Ana, California, and went for primary pilot training in Tucson, Arizona. He Married Evelyn Naglik in June of 1942.

He was reassigned to bombardier training in Deming, New Mexico, and also received navigation training there. As a second lieutenant, George was one of four officers on the B-17. He, Casey, Hank, and navigator Donald McPhee would form a special bond and spend many hours getting to know each other.

Walter Sybo

Walter Sybo, the flight engineer and top turret gunner, was born on April 8, 1924, in Pittsburgh, Pennsylvania. The fourth of eight children born to Stanley and Rose Sybo, he grew up in the Morningside neighborhood and graduated from Peabody High School in the Steel City. His two brothers also served in World War II, and his older brother John was killed a month before Walt and his crew were shot down. John was a crew member on a plane that crashed into a mountain while "flying the hump," the dangerous route over the Himalayan Mountains on which much-needed supplies were sent from India to forces fighting the Japanese in China.

Walt's younger brother Louis, a member of the army infantry, was about to board a ship for the Pacific theater when he learned that Walt was missing in action. Louis was immediately removed from active duty. A new federal law stipulated that if two members of a family were either killed or missing in action, any remaining members of the family in the military were not permitted to be on active duty. This law was enacted after the five Sullivan brothers went down together on their naval ship in the Pacific.

Donald McPhee

Donald McPhee was the all-important navigator of the B-17. His fellow crew members described him as being pleasant but quiet and introverted.

Through research I discovered that he was born in Canada on November 29, 1919, but that his family moved near San Francisco, California. He either joined the military or was drafted from the town of Burlingame, located between San Francisco and San Jose. For the most part, Don was described as Pleasant but reserved Scotchman who usually kept to himself. He was well suited for the navigator's responsibilities, having an aptitude for numbers and calculations, a talent that would later serve him well in civilian life.

Royce McGillvary

Royce McGillvary, a replacement waist gunner on B-17 crews in England, was born on April 27, 1923, in Gary, Indiana. He was the only child of Thomas and Olive McGillvary. His father worked in the steel industry in Gary, but after the stock market crash in 1929, he, like millions of Americans, lost his job. When Royce was seven years old, the family was forced to move to Nova Scotia, Canada, where his uncle owned a farm.

Royce graduated from St. Agnes High School in New Waterford, Nova Scotia, in 1941 and was inducted into the Canadian military and sent for pilot training with the Canadian Royal Air Force. He washed out and was sent to gunnery school in Saskatchewan.

After being sent overseas, he was given the opportunity to transfer to the American air force and was eventually assigned to the Ninety-Second Bomb Group, 407th Squadron. He was not assigned to a regular crew, and he had completed ten missions with others when fate brought him together with Hank and Casey's group.

Clayton Verlo

Clayton Verlo was born on August 4, 1921, in Madison, South Dakota. He was the only child of Aleck and Hilda Verlo, and because his father worked as a carpenter, his family moved often during his youth. The Verlos finally settled in Wisconsin where Clayton graduated from Gays Mills High School in 1939.

He enrolled in the LaCrosse Teachers College and completed one year of studies before enlisting in the Army Air Corps in 1940. Initially he trained as an aircraft mechanic at Chanute Field in Illinois before moving on to Lincoln Airfield in Nebraska where he received gunnery training. At Lincoln he met his future wife, a Nebraska girl named Lillian Tilly.

Seymour Wolfson

Seymour Wolfson was born in Wilkes Barre, Pennsylvania on October 24, 1915. He was the son of Sarah Plotkin Wolfson and Morris Wolfson. He would also live in California and settled in the Akron, Ohio area.

Irvin Sumpter

Irvin Sumpter was born on July 24, 1922, in Pawhuska, Oklahoma. He was the fourth of ten children born to Casper and Sena Sumpter. He graduated from Ramona High School and entered the Army Air Corps in September of 1942 in nearby Tulsa.

He received basic training at Shepherd Field in Texas and gunnery training in Harlingen, Texas, and went on to armament school at Lowery Field in Boulder, Colorado. He was initially trained as a gunner in A-20s at Will Rogers Field in Oklahoma and in Lake Charles, Louisiana. At Moses Lake and in Spokane, Washington, in 1943 he became part of the B-17 crew. Affectionately referred to as Sarge, he was a likable and capable part of the crew, manning the crucial tail gunner position.

Casimir Jerome "Casey" Paulinski

The Frederick Army Air Field

of

Frederick, Oklahoma

announces the graduation of

Class 43-G

Thursday morning, July twenty-ninth

nineteen hundred and forty-three

at nine o'clock

Post Theatre

Announcement of Aviation Cadet Training Class Graduation
From Frederick Army Airfield, Oklahoma

Aviator in training Casey Paulinski

Casey and fellow Aviation Cadets

The B-17 Crew together while training stateside.
(L-R, Back) Walter Sybo, Clayton Verlo, William Anderson
Hubert O'Neill, Seymour Wolfson, Irvin Sumpter
(Front) Henry Roeber, Casey Paulinski, George Sokolsky, Donald McPhee

Casey with his parents, Eleanor and Adam Paulinski

B-17 Pilot Henry "Hank' Roeber

Aviation Cadet, B-17 Co-Pilot and Casey's friend, Arthur Pinzke

Hank Roeber and Casey Paulinski
Pilot and Co-Pilot

Radio Operator Hubert O'Neill

Replacement Waist Gunner Royce McGillvary

Tail Gunner Irvin Sumpter

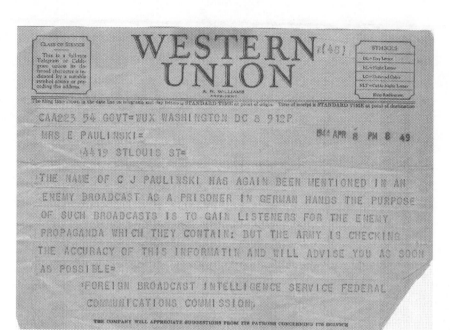

Telegram informing Casey's Family of German Radio
Broadcast mentioning Casey's Name

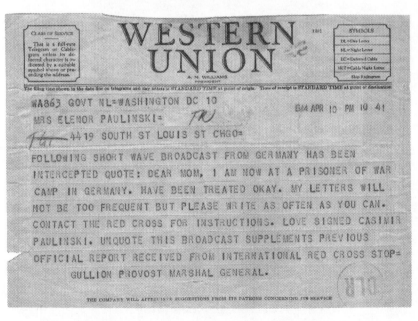

Telegram with message from Casey to his family

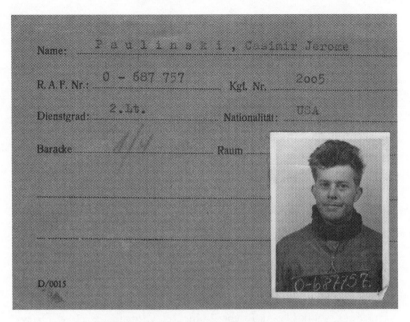

German POW Identification Card and Mug Shot of Casey

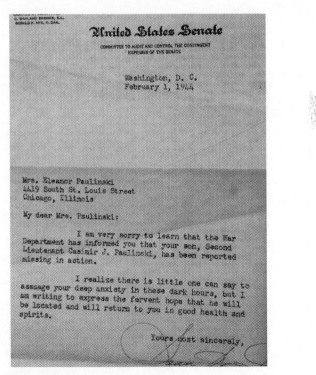

Letter from Illinois Senator Scott Lucas to Casey's Mother

Drawings by Pilot Hank Roeber in his Red Cross Issued POW Diary

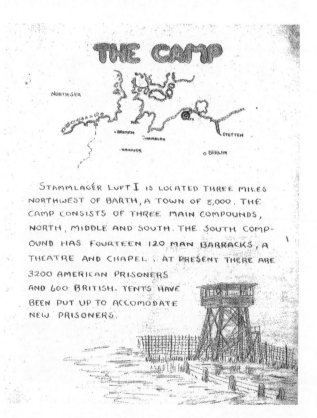

OUR TUNNELLING OPERATIONS ARE DISCOURAGED BY THE GERMANS, IN FACT, THEY TAKE EVERY PRECAUTION TO DETECT AND DESTROY EFFORTS OF SUCH A NATURE.

GUNNERS PRAYER

I WISHED TO BE A PILOT
  AND YOU ALONG WITH ME
BUT IF WE ALL WERE PILOTS
  WHERE WOULD THIS AIR FORCE BE ?
IT TAKES GUTS TO BE A GUNNER
  TO SIT OUT IN THE TAIL
WHERE THE MESSERSCHMIDTS ARE HOWLING
  AND THE SLUGS BEGIN TO WAIL
THE PILOTS JUST A CHAUFFER
  ITS HIS JOB TO FLY THE PLANE
BUT ITS WE WHO DO THE FIGHTING
  THOUGH WE NEVER GET THE FAME
SINCE WE ALL CAN'T BE PILOTS
  LET US MAKE THIS SOLEMN BET
WE'LL BE THE BEST DAMN GUNNERS
  THAT HAVE LEFT THIS STATION YET

THE GERMAN BREAD IS NOTORIOUS HERE FOR ITS
ACTION ON THE HUMAN SYSTEM. THE OPERATION
OF THE "HONEY" WAGON (SANITATION) IS NOTICED TO
BE IN DIRECT RELATION TO THE OPERATION OF
THE BREAD TRUCK.

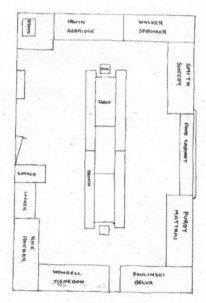

WE DO NOT SLEEP TWO IN A BED

10

RED CROSS PARCELS

ENGLISH	CANADIAN	AMERICAN
1 CAN CRACKERS	1 5oz CHOC BAR	1 BOX CRACKERS
1 CAN STEW	1 CAN SPAM	1 CAN SPAM
1 CAN MEAT ROLL	1 CAN CORNED BEEF	1 CAN CORNED BEEF
1 CAN FISH	1 CAN SARDINES	1 BOX RAISINS OR PRUNES
1 CAN EGGS	1 CAN SALMON	2 4oz CHOC. BARS
1 CAN CHEESE	1 BOX CRACKERS	1 CAN PATÉ
1 PK FRUIT	1 BOX PRUNES	1 CAN POWDERED MILK
1 CAN MARGERINE	1 BOX RAISINS	1 CAN SOL. COFFEE
1 12oz JAM	1 PK. COFFEE	1 CAN JAM OR ORANGE JUICE
1 2oz PK TEA	1 PK. SUGAR	1 BOX SUGAR
1 BAR SUGAR	1 16oz JAM	1 PK. CHEESE
1 4oz CHOC BAR	1 PK CHEESE	1 CAN MARGERINE
1 CAN BACON	1 CAN POWDERED MILK	2 BARS SOAP
1 CAN PUDDING	1 16oz CAN BUTTER	100 AMER. CIG'S
1 CAN COND. MILK	1 BAR SOAP	
1 CAN OATS	50 ENG. CIGS	
1 CAN COCOA		
1 BAR SOAP		
50 ENG. CIGS		

Casey and Russian Soldiers after Liberation from Germans

33

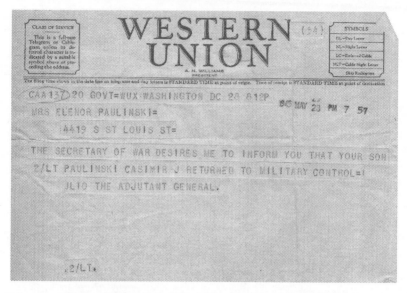

Telegram informing Casey's Family he has been returned to Allied Control

Mrs. Pieters lowering the Railroad Crossing Gates next to her property

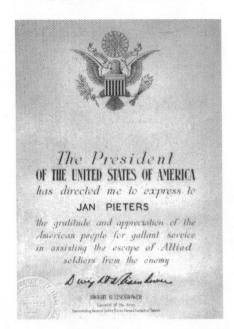

Letter of thank you from General Eisenhower

Photo of Casey he sent with Thank you Letter to Pieter's Family in the
Netherlands from Douglas Army Airfield, Arizona -October 1945.

Chapter 4

Training on the B-17 and then on to England

Hank Roeber was assigned to be the pilot of a B-17 Flying Fortress bomber, and the ten-man crew assembled at the army airfield at Moses Lake, Washington, in the summer of 1943. Here Hank met Casey Paulinski, who would be his copilot and a man he would rely on greatly to help mold a crew for combat across the Atlantic Ocean.

Hank described Casey as a likable, fun-loving guy with a quirky sense of humor. "He told us that after the war he was going to become an undertaker in Chicago. Now I don't know if this was true or if he was just pulling our leg," said Hank.

Hubert O'Neill, the youngest of the crew, who turned nineteen when the men went over to England in November of 1943, remembered the first time he met Hank Roeber and Casey Paulinski.

"I went to their tent and saluted Hank and Casey and introduced myself," he recalled. "Hank then said to me that this would be the first and last time that he expected me to salute him." Hubert would have the important responsibility of radio communications between each man on the crew and between airplanes.

As for training on this massive four-engine aircraft, Art Pinzke described landing a B-17 for the first time as "similar to landing your house from the second floor." The two pilots were that high up in the plane compared with their positions in smaller single- and twin-engine planes.

Every three days the crews would fly west over the Pacific Ocean and go on maneuvers, with the gunners taking aim at targets being towed in the ocean. This could be tedious work, but there wasn't time for extensive training due to the need for crews in England and elsewhere.

Hubert recalled pilot Hank Roeber turning over the controls to copilot Casey Paulinski to land the aircraft on one training flight.

"When Hank would land the aircraft it was usually very smooth, and you didn't really see much of the ground until we finally approached the landing strip.

"This one time Casey had control of the plane, and I noticed how close we were to the steeples of churches on the ground. Well, Casey brought us down more like a fighter pilot, and we bounced a few times on landing after which Casey came back and asked us how the landing was, and I joked, 'Which one?'"

It was not uncommon for bomber pilots and copilots to act like frustrated fighter pilots. This isn't surprising, because being a fighter pilot in a fast, sleek plane was far more romantic and exciting in the eyes of a young man than manning a much slower, hulking bomber. This was true of Casey, who had dreamed of being a P-47 or P-38 fighter pilot during his basic and primary training in cadet class 43-G.

Evenings on the base at Moses Lake and Geiger Field were usually spent writing letters home to loved ones and friends, playing cards, or catching up on reading. Life wasn't glamorous, but it sure beat having to spend the night in a tent at the mercy of the weather while on maneuvers as men in other branches of the armed forces had to do.

On one occasion in El Paso, Texas, when the crew was given a twenty-four-hour pass, an amusing incident occurred after a night on the town. One of the men passed out from one too many cocktails and was transported through a hotel lobby on a davenport. "It was the funniest thing you ever saw, carting him up through the halls and into the elevator on this piece of furniture," said Hubert O'Neill. George Sokolsky remembered that the men brought the davenport into an elevator and that the hotel supposedly had a difficult time getting it back down the following day.

The next morning as their crewmate recovered from a hangover, the men administered oxygen to give him a boost for an upcoming training flight.

A special event involving Clayton Verlo took place in Spokane. He and Lillian, the girl he met in Lincoln, Nebraska, were married on October 10, 1943, making Clayton the third man on the crew to tie the knot along with Hank Roeber and George Sokolsky.

After stops in El Paso, Texas, and Grand Island, Nebraska, the crew members eventually arrived in New York City for what would be the long trip across the Atlantic Ocean to England and their first taste of the war.

The crew left New York Harbor on November 6, 1943, aboard a converted British ship. The trip to England took five days. The ship went unescorted, taking a southerly course to avoid German U-boats. These guys from the Army Air Corps must have had a strange feeling being transported by boat rather than flying to England. But in November of 1943, there weren't enough bombers and other aircraft to go around.

After arriving in England and completing all the necessary processing, the men were assigned to the Ninety-Second Bomb Group, 407th Bomber Squadron, at an army airbase outside the small village of Podington, England. The Ninety-Second, nicknamed Fames Favored Few, was under the command of Col. William M. Reid when Hank and Casey's crew arrived in England. The Ninety-Second consisted of four squadrons—the 325th, 326th, 327th, and the 407th.

Podington was a small rural community fifty miles north of London in the far northwest corner of Bedfordshire. The Ninety-Second, part of the First Bombardment Division of the Eighth Air Force, had moved to Podington in mid-September of 1943 after being based in Bovingdon and Alconbury.

Just a few miles north of Podington was the town of Chelveston, home to the 305th Bomb Group. Those who grew up in Chicago in the 1960s and early '70s will remember Chevelston, a duck that frequently appeared on the live children's morning TV show Ray Raynor and Friends.

Most children didn't know that the duck had been named for the town in England where Raynor had served in the Army Air Corps as a B-17 navigator. Raynor and his crew were shot down, and he was sent to the well-known POW camp Stalag Luft 3 near Sagan, Poland. This was the site of the famous Great Escape recounted in the 1963 blockbuster movie with an all-star cast that included Steve McQueen, Richard Attenborough, and James Garner.

Raynor and his fellow American POWs were digging an escape tunnel, code-named Tom, Dick, and Harry, while British POWs were digging another, the one that would be used in the Great Escape. However, the German guards discovered the Americans' tunnel before it could be completed and shipped the Americans to another POW camp. I'll have more on Raynor later in the book.

Initially, Hank, Casey, and the others were assigned to more experienced crews for a couple of missions so they could learn the ropes in combat situations.

The men flew four combat missions before one fateful day a little more than a month after their arrival in England. These missions included Emden, Germany, on December 11; Kiel, Germany, on December 13, and Bremen, Germany, on December 16 and 20. The mission to Emden and the two to Bremen were to bomb port areas, and on the one to Kiel, the target was submarine pens.

George Sokolsky had the added responsibility of helping to review all correspondence the soldiers sent back home, and he would censor any references that might compromise military operations. Hubert O'Neill missed most of the flights with his mates due to a blister on his foot that became infected and forced him to be hospitalized.

O'Neill would, however, witness the terrible accident that would prove fatal to his crewmate and close friend from Massachusetts, Lawrence Anderson.

The crew's first scheduled mission, a run to La Rochelle, France, was scrapped due to poor weather. On the way back to the barracks from where the B-17s were parked, Anderson, who was hanging on to the side of a transport vehicle packed with returning airmen, apparently slipped off. He fell under the truck and suffered fatal injuries after being crushed by the wheels.

This was a devastating blow to the crew, which had trained together for many months and had grown close. Fellow Bostonian O'Neill was particularly hard hit. He had been riding in the truck and had witnessed the accident.

Lawrence Anderson died on December 7, 1943, the two-year anniversary of the attack on Pearl Harbor. He is buried at the US military cemetery in Cambridge, England.

Hank Roeber's first mission, acting as a copilot with a more seasoned pilot and crew, was on November 16, 1943. The Ninety-Second Bomb Group participated in a run to Knaben, Norway, to bomb the molybdenum mines. Of the 130 bombers from the First Bomb Division taking part, one aircraft from the Ninety-Second and Hank's squadron, the 407th, did not return. The aircraft piloted by 2nd Lt. Joseph Thornton was shot down, with all of the crew surviving and becoming POWs except the navigator, Staff Sgt. David Besbris, who evaded capture.

Three days earlier, a mission to Bremen was abandoned after only three hours in the air. One of the 407th's planes, piloted by Lt. Hiram Fisher, crashed and burned in Gaydon Village on its return to the base. All ten aboard the B-17 were killed.

Typically, twenty-five to thirty-five aircraft would be involved in a bomb group's mission. Many early missions would include three hundred to seven hundred aircraft, both bombers and fighter escorts from numerous bomb groups. Until January of 1944, however, fighter escorts such as P-47 Thunderbolts, P-51 Mustangs, and P-38 planes could accompany bombers only to points near the German border because of limited fuel capacity.

This would change when P-51s were equipped with additional drop tanks, allowing them additional fuel to fly deep into German territory. These "little friends" as the bomber crews called them, were much appreciated for their ability to fend off German fighter aircraft.

On November 26, ten days after his first mission, Hank again served as copilot, with Bremen's port the target. Bremen, a major target of Allied bombers, was well protected by antiaircraft artillery, and on this mission of the 440 bombers and 381 fighter planes that reached the objective, two Ninety-Second Bomb Group aircraft were shot down with more tragic results.

The aircraft piloted by 2nd Lt. Truman Shannon was last seen entering a cloud full of German fighters; all ten aboard were killed. Another B-17, piloted by 2nd Lt. Hugh C. Dougherty, was shot down, and seven of the ten men aboard, including Dougherty, were killed. Three of the crew survived and wound up becoming POWs. In total twenty-five bombers and four fighters from the Eighth Air Force were lost during this mission.

In addition to the lost crews and the fatalities, others suffered severe injuries including wounds from enemy gunfire, frostbite, shrapnel wounds from flak, and hypoxia from lack of oxygen.

On what was to be Hank's third and final mission with another crew, the target was an industrial area of Solingen, Germany. However, due to heavy cloud cover, the Ninety-Second Bomb Group and other First and Second Division groups were recalled after takeoff. Once again tragedy befell a Ninety-Second Bomb Group crew. The aircraft piloted by Capt. William Pugh crashed on takeoff, and all crew members were killed. This was particularly heartbreaking because most of them were flying what would have been their last or next-to-last mission before being sent home. Pugh had recently been named the commanding officer of the 327th Squadron.

Soilingen was again the target the next day, and yet another Ninety-Second Bomb Group crew suffered a disaster.

The B-17 piloted by 2nd Lt. George C. Hale received flak damage in its right wing and spun out of control. All were killed except tail gunner Donald Wilson, who was able to parachute out of the crippled aircraft. He was, however, captured and became a POW. Wilson, who was on his first mission, was subbing for the regular tail gunner, who was sick.

Hank, Casey, and the rest of the crew certainly got a baptism of fire and a grim dose of aerial combat reality before they flew together.

Art Pinzke recalled how exhausting it was to fly the B-17 in tight formation for more than eight hours. "We [the pilot and copilot] took turns flying the plane. No one could fly a plane that long by themselves," he said.

Pinzke also talked about a strange situation during flights. "You never heard the other planes, only the sound of flak when it was too close or hitting your own plane," he said. "It was eerie to see but not hear another plane exploding near you."

The ground crew, medical staff, commanding officers, and other military personnel would anxiously await the return of bomb group aircraft to the base, counting the B-17s as they landed. Medical teams were ready to treat and to transport the wounded from damaged aircraft, and ground crews had the grim task of removing the bodies of those who had been killed.

This could be a difficult and dangerous task, with fuel lines often damaged and intact bombs that hadn't been jettisoned remaining in the aircraft. Numerous ground personnel were injured or even killed near planes.

Immediately after returning to the base, crew members would go through a briefing with commanding officers, detailing what they saw and experienced on the mission and reporting success or failure in reaching and hitting the target. If an aircraft had been hit and had dropped out of formation or worse, surviving crewmen would explain in as much detail as they could recall or report anything they had managed to write down.

Base personnel would help crew members calm down by giving them a shot of whiskey. This created an uproar back in the States, particularly from the Women's Christian Temperance Union, which vigorously complained about the practice.

Typically, when a crew did not return, the remaining members of the squadron would look through the missing airmen's personal effects and prepare to send them to families back home. Items like cigarettes and chewing gum would be doled out to the remaining men. Belongings deemed overly sensitive or potentially classified would stay with the commanding officer.

The squadron's commanding officer would have the grim responsibility of writing a letter home to the airman's family expressing his deepest sympathies, particularly if the soldier had died in the line of duty, and giving as much detail as possible about the circumstances.

Between missions, life at an airbase was mundane and much of the time downright boring. The tiny village of Podington had few pubs or forms of entertainment. The closest town with a theater and a greater selection of pubs was Northampton, and crew availability and pending missions meant that passes were sometimes denied.

The British had a saying about the American fliers: "They're overpaid, oversexed, and over here." Numerous airmen indeed developed relationships with young British women, and some even wound up marrying.

Hank and Casey's crew was not in England long enough to have spent much time cultivating relationships in the villages. And of course Hank, Clayton, and George were already married.

I talked to numerous veterans about what Hollywood film best depicted life in the air corps in Europe, and to a man they said the 1949 Twentieth Century Fox movie *12 O'Clock High*, starring Gregory Peck and directed by Henry King, was the most accurate. Peck was nominated for an Academy Award for his role, and Dean Jagger won the Oscar for best supporting actor for his superb performance. The movie also featured outstanding performances by Hugh Marlowe, Gary Merrill, and Millard Mitchell.

The movie and Peck's character were based on events that had occurred with the 306th Bomb Group and the assigning of a new commanding officer (played by Peck). In the movie the bomb group is given the fictitious number 918th, which is 306 multiplied by three.

Chapter 5

Together as a Crew in Combat

With Hank Roeber at the controls and Casey Paulinski seated to his right as the copilot, their B-17 crew flew its first mission on December 11, 1943. The target was the port area of Emden, Germany. The crew included a replacement for Lawrence Anderson, who had died four days earlier.

Twenty aircraft began taking off at one-minute intervals at 0834 hours. Four-and-a-half hours later they reached the target area and released their bombs. All of these planes returned safely to the base at Podington, six with minor damage. However, of the 523 Eighth Air Force bombers in the attack force, seventeen did not return to their bases, and four of the 388 fighter planes also did not make it back.

Two days later a mission to bomb the submarine yards in Kiel, Germany, produced similar results. Again, no Ninety-Second Bomb Group aircraft were lost, but three of the 352 bombers in the strike force did not return, and two of the 394 fighter planes went missing in action.

On December 16 the commanding officer of the Ninety-Second, Col. William Reid, led a mission to Bremen. One of the crews did not make it back to the base. The aircraft piloted by Lt. Edward Walsh was last seen aborting inside enemy territory. Six of the crew, including Walsh, were killed, two evaded capture, and two became POWs. Ten of the 535 planes that made it to the target were listed as missing in action with one of the 201 fighter aircraft also going down.

Four days later the Ninety-Second again visited Bremen as part of a 472-bomber attack. One of the crews did not make it back to the base. German fighters shot down the B-17 piloted by 2nd Lt. Edward Cole. He and six others were killed in action, and three of the crew survived to become POWs. In all, twenty-seven bombers were shot down on this mission, accounting for more than 270 airmen.

By December 22, Hank, Casey, and the crew had participated in four missions that saw fifty-seven bombers and thirteen fighter planes shot down, accounting for 583 men from the Eighth Air Force. This was a staggering figure considering that it represented people who had possibly been killed or wounded, been taken prisoner, or were evading capture.

December 22, 1943. Target: Osnabruck, Germany

The primary target for the mission of December 22 was the railroad marshaling yards in Osnabruck, Germany. As usual the men were awakened about 4:00 a.m., with takeoff around 8:00 a.m.

In each of their previous missions, they had a different waist gunner taking the spot that Lawrence Anderson would have occupied. On this mission Sgt. Royce McGillvary took the position alongside Sy Wolfson.

The Eighth Air Force sent 346 B-17s and B-24s, and 234 made it to the target. The crew was flying in a borrowed B-17 named the *USS Aliquippa*. The plane, possibly paid for through a war bond drive by the town of Aliquippa, Pennsylvania, may have been named by its regular crew, probably the pilot. The *Aliquippa* had flown nineteen successful missions, as evidenced by the number of bombs painted on its left nose.

As the formations neared the target sometime around 1330 hours (1:30 p.m.), heavy cloud cover disrupted the full brunt of the attack. The flak was fierce, and the much faster German fighter planes, including but not limited to Messerschmitts (ME-109s and 110s) and Focke-Wulfs (FW-190s), were weaving in and out, shooting at the bombers.

After George Sokolsky had taken control of the aircraft at the target and dropped the bomb load, Hank followed the lead aircraft's direction and turned the *Aliquippa* back toward England. Suddenly the plane was hit by flak or a German fighter's machine-gun fire. Engine number four (on the outside right) was on fire, and the plane was losing altitude and dropped out of formation.

Hank and Casey did all they could to keep the aircraft under control, but suddenly engine number one (on the outside left) started smoking and went dead, also having been hit by flak or enemy fighter bursts. The plane was now at the mercy of German fighters.

Eyewitness accounts during debriefing in Podington were supplied by Staff Sgt. Clyde Hall, the tail gunner, and Staff Sgt. Daniel Williams, the ball turret gunner aboard the B-17 flying on Hank and Casey's left wing. They said that P-38s came to their rescue and were joined by a P-47 and that while Hank and Casey's plane was losing altitude, it seemed under perfect control. The crew fired green flares to signal trouble. Hall and Williams last saw the *Aliquippa* as it descended into the clouds.

Hank Roeber recalled a crucial decision that may have saved the crew from continued attack by the German fighters.

"You have to realize that the German fighters loved a single, crippled B-17, and we were a sitting duck, so I lowered our landing wheels as a sign of surrender," Hank said. "At that moment the American escort and German fighters peeled off and left us alone to our own devices."

Hank and Casey had to make a difficult decision. They could try to fly the plane with the entire crew, or they could ring the bailout bell and have most of the men jump into the frigid cold and face the consequences.

After conferring with Casey and flight engineer Walt Sybo, Hank made the gut-wrenching decision to ring the bell and order most of the crew to bail out.

Because they were somewhere near the German-Dutch border, the seven crewmen would be at the mercy of the Nazis or possibly hostile locals as they parachuted out.

Hubert O'Neill, who was the nineteen-year-old radio operator, remembered no outward panic when it came time to jump. "We were actually kind of joking around as to who would be the first to jump and so on," he said.

"You have to remember we had never trained to parachute, so this was our first and only time we would be doing it," Hubert said. "It wasn't like we were paratroopers who had done this multiple times in training and somewhat knew what to expect."

Royce McGillvary, the replacement waist gunner, recalled waving to navigator Donald McPhee from the front of the plane as they jumped out.

Bombardier George Sokolsky was the last of the seven men out. Before jumping, he maneuvered from his position in the nose of the aircraft to the back of the plane to make sure no one was left.

Hubert O'Neill had a scare when he pulled the ripcord. "I looked up and saw that there was a big hole in the top of the parachute," he recalled. "I thought I had torn it and was going to fall to my death. I then realized the hole was supposed to be there, and I lazily floated toward the ground." He was quickly captured by a group of German soldiers.

Clayton Verlo jumped through the clouds and landed in a farm field but evaded capture by burrowing into a haystack until nightfall.

"After it was dark I got out and saw a house. I did not hear any noises, so I spent the night in the barn," he said. "The next morning the farmer discovered me in the barn, and I started hiking in the general direction of England."

Hank, Casey, and Walt remained with the aircraft as it continued to lose altitude. Initially Hank wanted to head for Switzerland, a neutral country. However, he realized that would be impossible with two engines out, so he decided to try to make it back to England. There was one problem: he had no navigator.

"If I had to do it over again, I would have told Don McPhee to stay with us rather than bail out," said Hank about his navigator. The B-17 continued to lose altitude and fuel as the plane crossed above German-occupied Holland. It became painfully obvious that the three men would not be able to nurse the plane back to England and would have to try to land it in hostile territory."

"All three of us kept looking for some open fields where we could land the plane," Hank said. Finally they sighted farmland, and with only one engine now operating, Hank and Casey eased the lumbering B-17 down for an emergency belly-landing.

The *Aliquippa* had landed safely near the town of Bornebroek in the Netherlands, although at that point, Hank, Casey, and Walt were not sure if they were in Dutch territory or in Germany.

Sixteen-year-old Jan Bolscher was plowing a field on his family's farm when suddenly he saw an enormous aircraft hovering overhead as it made its way down for a landing. Bolscher remembered the B-17 flew right over him and the horses pulling the plow.

"The horses got terribly frightened and tried to bolt," Bolscher recalled in the book *In Verdrukking, Verzet en Vrijheid*, written by Dutch historian Henne Noordhuis about World War II in the Netherlands. The English translation of the title is *In Oppression, Resistance and Liberty*.

Bolscher remembered that the crewmen tried to destroy the plane by firing flares into it. However, they did not succeed, and the plane and its contents became prizes for the Nazis and the townspeople.

As the three Americans exited the aircraft, Bolscher motioned them toward a wooded area adjacent to the farm field where they could make their escape. This was good advice because shortly afterward, a German soldier driving a motorcycle with a sidecar arrived, with other soldiers soon to follow.

After hiding in the woods until nightfall, the three men found their way to railroad tracks, which they followed toward the town of Goor. They spent the night in a shed on what appeared to be a small farm.

Walter Sybo recalled seeing the wooden shoes of the owner, Jan Pieters the next morning and thinking, *Thank God we're in Holland.*

The family, which sheltered them, was part of the Dutch underground and offered Casey, Hank, and Walt the opportunity to link up with other members of the resistance. After securing civilian clothes, food, and Dutch money, the men decided to make their way toward the town on their own rather than put the family at risk of being arrested for harboring enemy soldiers.

The three men reached the center of town and eventually came into contact with townspeople and even German soldiers but initially were not suspected of being American soldiers.

In a diary that he dictated to his sister Joanne after the war, Casey recalled that they entered a church and tried to communicate with a priest. None of the men knew Dutch, and the priest did not understand English, so the three Americans tried their best to indicate who they were and what they wanted.

The priest motioned them toward a convent, and when the three men were able to make the nuns understand that they were looking for help, the nuns became frightened of the consequences and refused them entrance.

"It was plain to see they would be endangering their own lives if they took us in," said Casey of the encounter.

Hank recalled that the nuns motioned them toward what they thought was a church building. After scaling a fence, the men entered the building and found to their surprise that it housed German soldiers.

"We were a bit bold because we had this Dutch money and were very hungry and thirsty, so we proceeded to go over to an area that looked like a bar, and I, knowing how to speak a little German, ordered three beers," said Hank about these tense moments. "After pulling out this Dutch money, which we did not know the worth of, the bartender poured us each a stein of beer, and we quickly drank up and left."

Casey remembered their sheer desperation. "No one was eating much those days in Holland, because all the food was rationed, and we had no food stamps, but we were able to drink anything and everything." He admitted that they were too bold, allowing themselves to be seen in broad daylight.

Fate would catch up to the men on Christmas Day 1943 when they entered a restaurant-bar in the town of Zutphen, looking for food. Hank recalled that the proprietor went into a back room or a kitchen to prepare them something but was gone for a suspiciously long time.

"We figured that something was a bit fishy, especially with a large portrait of Adolf Hitler hanging on the wall, and quickly left." Once outside, however, they were confronted by a policeman on a bicycle, who announced that they were under arrest.

"The police officer said what fools we were to be walking around in broad daylight and that while he regretted having to arrest us, he had no choice but to turn us over to the German authorities," said Hank. Word had already spread among the townspeople and the German authorities that a downed American aircraft had been found and that the crew was probably somewhere in the area, trying to evade capture.

The three men were escorted to the Zutphen police station where they awaited the Germans. "Suddenly the door slammed open, and the Gestapo entered and grabbed us by our collars and practically dragged us out of the police station," Hank recalled.

Initially the fact that the men were not wearing American military uniforms and had discarded their dog tags put them in a life-threatening predicament.

"By rights, they could have immediately shot us as suspected spies," said Hank. Casey recalled that his situation was even worse because he was carrying a rosary with an attached medal that bore his full Polish name, Casimir Jerome Paulinski.

"They took it for granted that I was a European Pole and immediately decided to dispose of me by shooting me," said Casey. "After pleading with them to wait and find out, to make sure I was an American airman, I convinced them to take me to German high command where I was properly identified and given the third degree."

Over the next two days the men were transported by passenger train to the German interrogation center for airmen, Durchgangslager der Luftwaffe, or Transit Camp of the Luftwaffe, which POWs called Dulag Luft, in the town of Oberursel, thirteen kilometers north of Frankfort-am-Main, Germany. There they were put in separate prison cells. This would be the last time Walt Sybo saw Casey Paulinski.

Chapter 6

From Free Men to Prisoners of War

Dulag Luft was a camp covering about five hundred acres. From 1942 through 1944, more than thirty-nine thousand Allied airmen were processed as POWs at this camp. As many as sixty-five interrogators were working there when its population peaked in 1944. Most of the buildings' roofs were painted with large white letters spelling out *POW* so that Allied aircraft would not bomb or strafe the camp. Watchtowers were spaced around the camp at approximately hundred-yard intervals, and two barbed-wire fences ten feet apart stood twelve feet high with trenches and barbed wire on the ground between them. In addition to the guards in the towers, trained German shepherds prowled the outer boundaries. This was no Boy Scout camp.

Hank recalled being interrogated by the Germans at Dulag Luft. He said the interrogator, named Von Beck, was initially cordial as he asked basic questions, such as name, rank, and serial number. When Von Beck asked what version of the B-17 Hank had piloted, Hank said he didn't know. "You are the pilot," the interrogator replied. "How could you not know what type of plane you were flying?" Hank suggested that the Germans check it out for themselves. This enraged the German officer, who replied, "Why should we put our hands on that filthy airplane?" A guard then grabbed Hank by the collar and dragged him off to his cell.

Casey recalled that the POWs were put in cold, dark cells with nothing to do, to see, or to hear for up to twenty-four hours a day. As for food, they were given only two paper-thin slices of bread each day in hopes of breaking them down to obtain information.

The interrogators at Dulag Luft were highly trained in ways to extract information from the young, scared airmen. Psychologists studied each prisoner to determine which method would break down his resistance.

Many of the POWs would be lulled into a false sense of complacency and could slip up and give important information. Those who showed signs of fear or who appeared overly nervous might be threatened with all kinds of torture, some of which was indeed carried out. Others were tempted with bribes, such as cigarettes, food, and clean clothes.

In one instance Casey accepted a cigarette, which had a strange effect on him. "After taking a puff or two, it struck me that it might be a doped one when I began to feel lightheaded and queasy," he said. "I threw it in the guard's face … [He] did his best to reassure me that it was okay. I picked it up and saved it for another puff later on and came to the conclusion that after not smoking for a long time and lack of food maybe that was the effect it had on me."

The men had been trained on what to expect if they were captured and interrogated. But even with this training, the German interrogators were quite skilled in extracting information from them.

While at Dulag Luft, Casey was allowed to write a short letter to his family, although by the time the Paulinskis received it in April of 1944, they had already been notified that he was a POW. The note read, "Dear Mother, just letting you know I am okay. I am not injured. Will write more soon as I am able. Please do not worry about me. My whole crew made it okay, all alive. More details to follow. Happy New Year! Casey."

After approximately a week, Casey, Hank, and other POWs were taken to the rail depot in Uberursel and put on a train to be shipped to their next destination. Walt Sybo did not accompany them. He was on his way to a different POW camp where three other members of his crew would join him.

Hubert O'Neill and Sy Wolfson were quickly captured upon landing in enemy territory and were eventually transported to Stalag 17B, which would be immortalized in the 1953 movie *Stalag 17*, starring William Holden in an Oscar-winning performance, with Otto Preminger, Peter Graves, and Sig Rumann, and directed by Billy Wilder. The two men arrived at the POW camp on December 30. They would mark the new year in less-than-festive circumstances.

Clayton Verlo evaded capture for a few days after parachuting out of the plane.

"I landed in a field and struggled to get my parachute off," said Clayton. "I ran in the direction of England and eventually burrowed myself into a haystack until it was dark. After it became dark, somewhere around 4:00 p.m., I saw a house, and not hearing any commotion, went into the barn and spent the night until the next morning when the farmer discovered me. I could tell he was afraid to have me anywhere near his property, so I started hiking across a field until I came across another farmer, who recognized my flying suit and took me to another building of a man named Krusinga, who was a notary, similar to a judiciary position in America."

Unfortunately for Clayton, everyone in the town knew he was there. Officials had a doctor examine him in hopes of finding something physically wrong so they could put him in a hospital instead of having to surrender him to the Nazis. "If they could just get me into a hospital, it was a lot easier to get a person out and hide him with the Dutch underground," Clayton said. On Christmas Eve he was taken to the town of Zwolle and put in a stone dungeon in solitary confinement.

He stayed there for almost a week and was questioned every day by Gestapo officers. While they never physically abused him, they peppered him with snide remarks about being a POW. He did, however, receive a kind parting gesture in the form of a cake, baked for him by Mrs. Krusinga. He didn't receive any cakes from the Nazis.

George Sokolsky and Donald McPhee were quickly captured after parachuting out of the aircraft and were eventually transported toward the Baltic Sea and the town of Barth, Germany, Casey and Hank's destination.

The news that the crewmen had been shot down reached their families about a week later in the form of the dreaded Western Union telegram. Then came official letters from the War Department informing the families that their loved ones were listed as missing in action.

Casey's family also received a letter of concern from US Senator Scott Lucas of Illinois, expressing his "fervent hope that he will be located and will return to you in good health and spirits." Another stark reminder for Casey's family was the Christmas cards and letters that the Army Air Corps sent back; he never had the chance to read them.

At about the same time Casey, Hank, and Walt were temporarily evading capture, Royce McGillvary and Irvin Sumpter were together after parachuting to the ground. They evaded capture for a few weeks with the help of the Dutch and later the Belgian underground, then decided to split up. Sumpter was captured by the Gestapo on April 18, 1944, and was first held at St. Gilles Bastille in Brussels, Belgium, for four months. This, however, was far from Sumpter's final stop during his time as a POW. McGillvary was captured in Belgium some six months later and sent to a Belgian Prison. However, it would he would experience another adventure shortly after.

The trip from Dulag Luft took about three days and was nerve-wracking because the POWs didn't know their final destination. Casey remembered traveling by rail and being put in town jails at night or before changing trains. "I still cannot stand the sound of trains, and nights are filled with nightmares," he said after the war. "I awaken frightened each time the trains ride past or uncouple or their whistles blow."

Stalag Luft 1 was their destination, and on January 7, 1944, when the four officers arrived, the camp had only a few hundred POWs. By war's end it would hold some ten thousand. Sokolsky and McPhee roomed together in the same barracks; Casey and Hank were also together, although in different bunks. Casey and Hank were in the south compound, while Donald and George were placed in the north compound.

Word of the crew being taken prisoner was relayed back to the families in the first week of February by Western Union telegram from the War Department, which had received the news from the Red Cross and through monitoring of German radio broadcasts, which announced the names of new POWs.

In addition to telegrams and official letters from the War Department, Casey's family received postcards from individuals who monitored foreign shortwave radio transmissions. The cards came from people as far away as Pennsylvania, Ohio, and Michigan who had heard that Casey was listed as German prisoner of war.

One of those who sent a postcard was E. E. Alderman of Dayton, Ohio, who wrote, "I have relayed over four thousand short wave radio messages to anxious families across the United States over the past two years, picked up from foreign stations."

A telegram dated February 27, 1944, from the Foreign Broadcast Intelligence Service of the Federal Communications Commission reported, "The name of second lieutenant Casimir J. Paulinski has been mentioned in an enemy broadcast as a prisoner in German hands. The purpose of such broadcasts is to gain listeners for the enemy propaganda which they contain, but the army is checking the accuracy of this information and will advise you as soon as possible."

A far more personal shortwave broadcast message was sent on April 10, 1944, via telegram, which said, "Dear Mom, I am now at a prisoner of war camp in Germany. Have been treated okay. My letters will not be too frequent, but please write as often as you can. Contact the Red Cross for instructions. Love, signed Casimir Paulinski."

After spending time in a Belgian prison, Irvin Sumpter was transported to Dulag Luft and then with other POWs was sent by cattle car to Stalag Luft 4 in Gross Tychow, Poland, near the Baltic Sea. Eventually he and other POWs would make the long, arduous journey southwest to Stalag 13D in Nuremberg, Germany.

With Allied forces approaching and after numerous air raids, on April 3, 1945, Sumpter and other POWs were forced to march toward Stalag 7A in Moosburg, Germany, just north of Munich. The more-than-hundred-mile trek was difficult and in a notable number of cases deadly. Sumpter spent the remainder of the war in Stalag 7A. The camp was liberated on April 29 by troops from Gen. George S. Patton's Third Army. Patton later toured the facility. By the time of the liberation, the camp, designed for fourteen thousand POWs, held more than 130,000, and living conditions had become deplorable.

In their book *The Last Escape: The Untold Story of Allied Prisoners of War in Europe 1944-45*, John Nichol and Tony Rennell described the POW experience: "Some sailed blithely through prison-camp life and returned home unaffected. Others were tormented for the rest of their lives. Such was the nature of camp life that one man's experiences could be totally at odds with those of a man in another hut, let alone the next compound of another camp hundreds of miles away."

In researching this book, I solved a mystery that my wife, Diane, and her sisters had wondered about for years. Casey had often spoken glowingly about one of his war buddies, someone he called "my paisan." Diane didn't know the man's name or any details about him. With the help of Hank Roeber's war diary, I learned that this person was Francis Belva, an airman from Rochester, New York, who shared a double bunk with Casey until suddenly being sent to different barracks after an escape tunnel was discovered.

Hank, who also roomed with Casey, recalled the boredom of camp life, the frigid cold, and the lack of solid food. This situation was common in all the POW camps, although conditions varied from one to the next, depending on who was in charge.

Another POW at Stalag Luft 1 was a British airman who would make a name for himself after the war as a movie actor. In a case of life imitating art, Donald Pleasence would co-star in the blockbuster POW movie *The Great Escape*, playing the role of Colin "The Forger" Blythe. He also was a technical adviser on the film and later would play a German executioner in the made-for-TV sequel, *The Great Escape II: The Untold Story*.

In another strange twist, he played the leader of the Gestapo, Heinrich Himmler, in the film *The Eagle Has Landed*. Himmler ordered the secret murder/execution of fifty of the escapees from Stalag Luft 3.

Initially, conditions at Stalag Luft 1 were almost bearable, according to Casey's memoirs. Parcels from the Red Cross came frequently enough, at first on a weekly basis, and the food, while certainly nothing like the meals back at the base in England, let alone at home, was adequate. Still, most people today would not consider eating much of what the Germans supplied.

Take, for instance, the "Kriegie" bread. While it may have been hearty, one would never see this bread in a bakery or a grocery store. The bread was a mixture of rye grain, sugar beets, tree flour (another way of saying sawdust), minced leaves, and straw baked into dark, coarse loaves. Many times POWs would find a surprise in the bread—broken glass, sand, and even mice or rat droppings.

Hubert O'Neill recalled discovering a surprise one day in the soup served to the POWs at Stalag 17B. "When we first got to the camp, I saw something swimming in the soup. It was maggots," he said. "As I was about to pluck it out of the soup and discard them, one of the guys who had been there awhile told me to eat them because it wouldn't kill me and would be the only protein that I would get."

One day when the POWs were given horse meat, O'Neill got another surprise. "I bit into this piece of meat and discovered a bullet, which was shocking at first, but then I felt better knowing that the poor animal had at least suffered a somewhat quick death," he said.

After being fed potatoes and then turnips for months on end, Casey was absolutely sick of them for years. "If it hadn't been for the Red Cross parcels, we would have starved to death," he said.

He received his first package from home some ten months into his captivity, and it lasted only an hour. Two more parcels arrived in October and November 1944, one containing pancake mix, which was a "real treat."

Casey used his ingenuity to concoct syrup for the pancakes. He scraped off the mold from some discarded prune pits. "I cooked them with some water," he recalled, "which created a sort of syrup, which we poured over the pancakes. What a feast!"

Casey recounted another example of creative cooking. "Some of our other successful and not-so-successful adventures in good eating were potato pancakes made of mashed potatoes, which turned into a mess," he recalled. "After that, we used raw potatoes. We also made a form of chocolate pudding by saving raw potato peelings and soaked the starch out of them and combining it with cocoa powder and powdered milk from our Red Cross parcels. That wasn't so bad."

The POWs were allowed to write short letters home, and their families were encouraged to write back. In a letter dated January 14, 1944, Casey wrote, "It has been pretty cold in this country, seen a little snow too. Please don't worry about me; I am in good health and good spirits."

The letters home were funneled through the Red Cross, so it usually took months for correspondence to make it from a POW camp in Germany across the Atlantic Ocean to America. Casey's family in Chicago didn't receive his first letter until April 10.

While most of the letters received from home were of a concerned, thoughtful nature, not all of them were encouraging. In fact, in his YMCA-issued diary, Hank Roeber wrote that many were downright nasty.

One airman received a sweater from a woman through the Red Cross. After sending this stranger a letter of thanks, he received a follow-up note from her. "I am sorry to hear that a prisoner of war received the sweater. I intended it for a fighting man," she wrote, as if his POW status had somehow stripped him of his dignity as a soldier. In another case, a POW received a letter from his father with whom he obviously had long-standing issues. "I knew I should have kept you at home and joined the Air Corps myself," said the not-so-loving parent. "Even when you were a kid I expected you to end up in prison."

Numerous men received "Dear John" letters from girlfriends, fiancées, and wives. After being in the camp for some three years, one Royal Air Force sergeant received this scathing version from his fiancée. "You can consider our friendship at an end. I'd rather be engaged to a 1944 hero than a 1941 coward."

Many of the letters were quite comical, owing to the fact that some of the people back home didn't quite understand the men's circumstances. One man's wife wrote, "Do you get to town very often?" Another penned this gem: "We are not sending you any parcels; we hear you can buy all you need in the stores near your camp."

Hank Roeber's diary is a treasure trove of detailed information about life at Stalag Luft 1, and like many others with an inordinate amount of time on their hands, he also exhibited wonderful artistic and poetic talent. The diary is chock-full of sketches, cartoons, and prose that is a fascinating read and an invaluable resource for this story.

Art Pinzke makes an unscheduled appearance

On March 22, 1944, Casey wrote home about a friend who had unexpectedly arrived at the camp. This pilot from Casey's cadet classes and his squadron in England had been shot down during the first successful Allied mission to Berlin.

Arthur Pinzke and his B-17 crew were shot down on March 6, 1944, on what was his fifteenth mission. This important Eighth Air Force mission included 730 bombers. The 504 B-17 and 226 B-24 bombers were dispatched to Berlin and surrounding targets.

Art's B-17 was one of sixty-nine bombers shot down that day, accounting for 690 men killed or missing in action. One of those killed was the pilot of his plane, 1st Lt. Elmyran R. Cooper, who died while trying to parachute out of the aircraft. His parachute got caught in the undercarriage of the B-17, probably the ball turret.

Art recalled how they were shot down. "We had dropped our bomb load and were well on our way over Holland, maybe ten minutes from the North Sea, heading for home, when we may have gotten a little careless," he said. "I was at the controls, and we were flying back toward the North Sea and England when suddenly a German fighter came out of the bright sunlight. The fighter shot us up, causing the plane to catch fire and forcing us to bail out." All crew members except Cooper safely parachuted out.

Casey's family saved Chicago newspaper articles about Art Pinzke being shot down and listed as missing in action and later as a POW. Before Art arrived at Stalag Luft 1, Casey suggested in his letters home from the camp that Art be contacted regarding his belongings back in England.

Art vividly recalled seeing Casey as he and other new POWs were marched into the camp. "Casey had this chagrined look on his face of 'welcome to our new home away from home' as he waved to me from behind the barbed- wire fence and said "Hi Ya." Unfortunately, this would be the last they saw each other in the camp, because Pinzke was placed in a barracks in the north compound.

As the spring of 1944 approached, warmer weather was an enticing vision for all of the POWs, who had suffered through freezing conditions in what Casey described as "the thoroughly ventilated barracks from all sides." He said that "when it snowed or rained it blew in from all sides, so with one pair of shoes and few socks, our feet were constantly wet and cold."

These conditions were compounded by standing at attention for roll call in raw weather at least twice a day, a ritual that could take hours.

"There wasn't a man there, including myself, whose arms and legs weren't frozen to the elbows and knees," said Casey about the effects of the cold. "Mine were like balloons most of the time, and I don't understand how we didn't lose them to frostbite."

The sleeping conditions were abominable. "The mattresses were made of wood shavings, and we were slowly being eaten up by vermin of every sort," Casey recalled. "There wasn't a spot on my body that wasn't chewed raw."

Conditions were similar to the south at Stalag 17B in Austria. In an audiotape that Clayton Verlo recorded for his daughter, he recounted how he wound up losing a considerable amount of weight by the time he was liberated.

POWs at Stalag Luft 1 and Stalag 17B never suffered from the severe overcrowding and deplorable conditions that prisoners like Irvin Sumpter faced at the end of the war at Stalag 7A in Moosburg. The camp, built to house fourteen thousand men, held 130,000 by 1945. Conditions were also horrific at Stalag 11B in Fallingbostel where POWs faced virtual starvation for months.

Toward the end of the war, POWs deemed healthy enough were forced to march from Stalag 17B, evacuating the camp as Allied troops advanced. The German military used this tactic in a number of instances, and thousands of men suffered greatly from starvation, frostbite, hypothermia, and exhaustion.

Walter Sybo, Seymour Wolfson, Hubert O'Neill and Clayton Verlo were among some four thousand participants in that forced march, and Clayton remembered vividly the details of this torturous trek. On April 8, 1945, they began the eighteen-day march, which covered 481 miles, to a camp near the town of Branau, Austria. More than nine hundred of the POWs from Stalag 17B were left behind in hospitals and would be liberated by Russian forces on May 9.

Verlo recounted the forced march in detail. "The Germans could hear the rumble of Russian Artillery in the distance and decided to evacuate the Camp. We marched for about 2-3 Hours each day for roughly 280 miles." "There were three of us from the Crew, Wolfson, Sybo and myself and we each had a blanket and overcoat to keep warm." "When we would sleep at night in open fields, we would sleep three together, Sybo, Wolfson and I laying close to each other to conserve heat, with each taking turns in the middle."

He recounted that most of the German guards were older soldiers, probably World War I Veterans, and they like the POW's wanted to rest as often as them. After being issued each a Red Cross parcel, which was supposed to last a about seven days, Food and water started to become scarce.

"We got ahold of some bad water. Was it given to us purposely by the German?' or was it safer for them because they were used to drinking it?" "It had something in it that gave us a form of dysentery."

Verlo recalled marching by the Mauthausen Concentration Camp, where Polish and Russian Prisoners were held. "It was a pitiful sight, the prisoners were so painfully thin like 10-12 year olds, but had aged and looked more like 70-80 years old." Vero recalled. "They really treated the Russians horrible, but we have learned that the Russians treated the Germans equally horrible."

After the Red Cross Parcels were used up, many POW's turned to trading with Austrian civilians. The more skilled were able to secure hand axes which would come in handy when they were forced to cut down pine trees for shelter in a wooded area next to a former Russian POW camp near Braunau, Austria.

"The shelters were good for a while until it rained, and then not particularly beneficial." Said Verlo about the make-shift conditions. Word also spread that President Roosevelt had Died and that Harry Truman was now President.

The infamous Bataan Death March in the Philippines is much more widely known. One of the survivors was Mario "Motts" Tonelli, a former University of Notre Dame and Chicago Cardinals football player. I was fortunate to know and to work with Motts in Chicago and to hear him recount the horrors he and other POWs faced while being forced to march to the encampment or while being held captive by Japanese forces.

Out of deep respect for all those who suffered and died, I will not try to compare numbers to determine which tragedies were worse. However, the forced marches in Europe have received significantly less notoriety despite the fact that many suffered and died or were left with scars for the rest of their lives. Fortunately, the POWs at Stalag Luft 1 did not face a forced march.

The POW's of Stalag 17B were finally liberated by American Troops on May 3, 1945 when six men of the 13th Armored Division arrived in jeeps and easily captured the remaining guards that hadn't already fled the camp. "We were finally Free, and I left the camp and found a farm where I liberated a Goose, which we had to eat," recalled Verlo. "The Army tried to feed us but wasn't prepared at that point."

May 7th they turned on the camps loudspeakers and we heard the Voice of Winston Churchill say "The War is Over!" Two days later the POW's were finally evacuated from a nearby Luftwaffe airfield by air on C-47 transports to France.

Chapter 7

Digging the Escape Tunnels

When the POWs weren't sleeping, in roll call, or keeping themselves busy with a variety of activities, many were secretly digging tunnels under the barracks in an attempt to escape.

Casey and Hank did their share of tunnel digging or acted as lookouts to warn the tunnel workers that guards were approaching. "We were all involved in digging tunnels at one time or another," Hank said.

"We planned this elaborate project, which was almost realized, though it may not seem possible that such a scheme could be executed right under the very noses of our guards," said Casey. "We held meetings, made plans, and drew maps for the digging of our tunnel and our eventual escape. Volunteers were recruited for the arduous task of digging a tunnel in less-than-ideal conditions, which posed some formidable obstacles and challenges."

One of the obstacles was that the barracks were elevated to make escape difficult. "We went into a hole through our floor," Casey recalled. "Each day we unscrewed the floorboards to go down and screwed them back up again. We dug up a plot of grass under the floor deep enough and in a blanket so that we could cover up boards we placed over the hole with it. We had to use special precautions to cover the hole in such a way that their dogs wouldn't be able to scent us when they walked beneath our barracks."

"We couldn't wear our uniforms underground, because they would get dirty and raise suspicion from the guards. So we instead stored our long underwear in the tunnel, and that was our work uniform," Casey said. "We stripped and donned them each time we went under, which was about five or six feet down."

The men quickly found out that because of a lack of air they couldn't stay down long. This necessitated the creation of some sort of air apparatus.

"We saved up all the food cans and made a sort of pipe and added them on as we progressed, along with a man pumping forced air from a barracks bag," said Casey. "We also had food down there if a man got hungry while digging so he didn't have to crawl back up. As for obstacles encountered while digging, once while digging they hit water, which had to be drained while they lay in the mud."

Digging was a dangerous, dirty, and claustrophobic experience with no guarantee of success. But the men continued, working around the clock when they could. As for disposing of the dirt, the men had a number of ingenious ways of getting rid of the evidence.

"As one man would dig out the dirt with a tin can, dirt would be poured into another can attached to a string, which was handed from one man to another until it was removed from the tunnel," said Casey. "The other men carried it out in their pockets and deposited it in the latrines or else tossed it up onto the roofs of our barracks. All this time the latrine was filling up with dirt, and the guards were searching for the opening to the tunnel because they knew the dirt wasn't growing there, but it was so well concealed they couldn't find it.

"Several times they ordered us out of the barracks while they searched high and low, but we were so well concealed they couldn't find it—that is, until one such time when we didn't have enough time to dispose of a bag of dirt, which they found in the guys' lockers."

The tunnel took approximately five months to dig and covered some eighty feet, almost to the other side of the barbed-wire fence. "We were to break out in two days, having only twenty more feet to go to safely be in the clear in the woods," said Casey. "We had everything in readiness, including Nazi and civilian uniforms, which one of the guys who was a tailor had made over from English and American soldiers' uniforms. We had money, food, and were prepared to go when our plans fell through. After all that tedious and monotonous work, it was heartbreaking."

In addition to the main tunnels being built in different barracks, the men dug "leaders" to detour the German guards if they ever went down after the prisoners.

Did the Germans know that the POWs were digging escape tunnels? By many accounts, probably. They considered this a good way to keep the prisoners busy until a tunnel was nearing completion. Then they would collapse the tunnel and flood it with water or worse, with sewage. Did the prisoners realize that the Germans knew what was going on? They probably did, but they were likely playing a game of cat and mouse, trying to outsmart their captors. In the case of the Great Escape from Stalag Luft 3, the British POWs were indeed able to outsmart the Germans, with some eighty men making it out of the camp, though at a terrible price for those executed by the ruthless SS.

By the time the tunnel that Casey, Hank, and the others had created was discovered, they had created an air tube consisting of more than three thousand tin cans. The Germans punched holes in the tops and the sides of the cans to prevent them from being used again.

The supply of food in tin cans lasted only as long as the Red Cross parcels and those from the POWs' families slowly made their way to the camps. As advancing Allied troops destroyed railroad lines, bridges, and roads after the D-Day invasion, conditions became increasingly difficult, and food supplies dwindled along with the tin cans.

The tunnel having been discovered, the men in the barracks were split up on January 26, 1945, and sent to other barracks and rooms. Hank and Casey were separated, but Hank and Francis Belva, would stay together for the duration of their confinement, though in a more cramped barracks.

Chapter 8

Food or a Facsimile Thereof

The POWs showed remarkable ingenuity, even creating makeshift distilleries from leftover cans. Casey recalled that each barracks seemed to have one but that the still in his quarters was a real dandy. "We had prune or raisin wine most of the time," he said, "but occasionally someone got a yen for something stronger, so we distilled whiskey, at least ninety proof."

The product didn't last long. "The men spent whole nights distilling it, but it was licked up as soon as a drop-full, so they had nothing to show for their labor," Casey said. "Heat was provided by oleomargarine of which we always had more than we could use, usually one pound per person provided by the Red Cross. We also used this to provide a source of light in the tunnels."

Casey was particularly noted for his fudge. "I made enough for Christmas to supply the eighteen men in our barracks for two days," he recalled. "I made it of powdered milk, English cocoa, and sugar."

The barracks baker remembered one major letdown. "My greatest disappointment came when I received a food parcel from home containing flour and proceeded to make us a cake. After preparing all the ingredients, I went to open the tin marked 'Basking Powder' only to find out that it was instead sugar. I couldn't console myself after such great expectations."

As the food supply diminished and starvation loomed, the men resorted to other extremes, such as catching and eating cats that had the misfortune of making their way into the camp.

"While they lasted, the cats made for good eating, and let me tell you they don't taste all that bad, just like rabbits," said Casey about this unique form of cuisine. "We tried trapping sparrows, but not having a morsel of food to tempt them with, [it] was a tedious and tiresome task waiting for them to come near enough to catch or to spot one who was curious enough to explore our trap and pounce on it."

As the war steadily turned in the favor of the Allied forces, the situation of the German people grew far worse, and so did conditions in the camp.

"Hunger is desperation, and we were becoming a desperate lot," said Casey. "Men went mad; others committed suicide, although no one actually died from starvation. I must have been the biggest optimist there, because I kept repeating, 'It won't be long now,' and tried to convince those around me and myself."

Casey said one British POW, a surgeon, had slowly gone insane after spending almost five years in prison camps since being captured early in the war in North Africa. "I guess he was offering hundreds of cigarettes to the boys if they would only allow him to perform appendectomies on them, just to give him something to do," Casey said. "The tragic part is that this doctor had no little or no medical supplies and could do little for the many men who had been shot down and suffered from neglected wounds, like shattered of shot-off limbs."

"If you were a POW, you didn't notice the gradual shrinking of each other's bodies from malnourishment. If we didn't see a guy for a couple of weeks, it was amazing how unrecognizable he would be," Casey said.

Casey and others had sympathy for the German guards and the civilians who worked in the camp and were also starving. "Don't let anyone tell you the German army is fed or clothed well," he said. "They were starving and freezing just as we were."

While over at Stalag 17B ...

Conditions were similarly unpleasant for Clayton Verlo, Hubert O'Neill, Walt Sybo, and Seymour Wolfson at Stalag 17B, and as the tide turned and Allied forces advanced into Germany and neighboring countries like Austria, prisoners at their camp and most others faced the prospect of evacuations and forced marches.

Stalag 17B was located near the town of Krems in northeast Austria near the border with Germany. Some four thousand men were held there, and conditions were comparable to those at other camps. The main difference was that near the end of the war most of the POWs, at least those physically able, were forced to make a long, difficult journey by foot in the bitterly cold winter.

The journey to the camp a year and a half earlier had also been harsh. Clayton Verlo recalled being transferred along with Walter Sybo from Dulag Luft like cattle in freight cars and standing or sitting on the cold floor of a rail car. Upon arriving at Stalag 17B, the POWs had their hair cut short by the Germans and were sent into a shower while their clothes were run through gas to remove any lice.

In all of the POW camps, a roll call of prisoners was held every morning, with prisoners from each barracks lining up separately and the men standing four deep. Clayton remembered a trick that the men would pull on the Germans. "One row would take half a step in one direction or the other, and that would mess up the count," he said. "This forced them to start the count over, which was very frustrating."

The men in Stalag Luft 1 and Stalag 17B had diversions that kept them busy including an orchestra and library, with instruments and books donated by the Red Cross. They also had sports, including baseball, and even put on musical productions, with the POWs playing both the male and the female roles. Donald Pleasance was involved in a number of these productions and would put this acting experience to good use in his successful career after the war.

The POW's and Guards also played a sort of game of Cat and Mouse mind game with each other. Verlo recalled on instance where a POW sat slowly sharpening the blade of his knife within view of a guard. The guard became increasingly uncomfortable until he finally had enough and asked to be sent to another part of the camp. Another time the Prisoners put a piece of toilet paper on an unsuspecting guards rifle bayonet like a flag. He continued marching back and forth as the POW;s and even a fellow German guards had a good laugh. That was until an officer reprimanded the guards.

In other instances a German Guard would purposely bump POW's in the stomach to instigate them, but nothing came of it.

And Finally They Were Free and No Longer Prisoners of War?

Liberation for the POW's at Stalag Luft 1 took place over a period of about two weeks at the end of May, 1945 when The Commandant apparatnely had orders from the German High Command to march the POWs out of Barth and away from advancing Russian troops. However the American Senior Officer, Colonel Hubert Zemke, a well regarded Fighter Pilot, told the Commandant that the POW;s would be ordered to resist any attempts to force them to march.. Fortunately, there was no bloodshed as late that evening the German guards were seen marching out of the camp leaving that gates unlocked.

Colonel Zemke and other officers than took over the camp, assigned Military Police to maintain order and to prevent local townspeople from entering. Contact Parties from both the British and American Officers were then sent to find the Russian Troops and after a few days scouting parties visited the camp and made arrangements for food to be provided for the now free airmen.

It has been written in various accounts that the Russians had threatened to move the POW's towards Odessa in Russia, but negotiations occurred for Allied Troops to hand over a renegade Russian Officer who had joined forces with the Germans and had been later captured by American forces.

The Allied Commanders than arranged for a mass evacuation by air on May 12th with stripped down Bombers ferrying former POW;s every few minutes, a Plane landing and quickly loading "Passengers" and than quickly taking off. This lasted over a couple of days. from a local airfield back to France.

Once in friendly territory, the POW's were examined, with the more ill being transported to military hospitals, while others were debriefed and finally fed and clothed as they waited to finally be shipped back home.

Royce McGillvary was ultimately the most successful of the crew in evading capture, despite being caught and spending time in a Belgian Prison. In what was a classified debriefing document from September, 1944, after Sumpter and McGillvary went their separate ways, McGillvary was aided by the Dutch Underground and then taken across the border into Belgium by a 23 old Dutch woman. He stayed for several weeks in Brussels with resistance fighters and than moved to the village of Wepion from the first week of February until June of 44'.

But his luck would run out on July 6th when he was being transported by truck along with three other evades to a wooded area when they were suddenly stopped and searched by a German motorcycle patrol. They were wearing civilian clothes and initially thought of as spies. After being transported to Brussels and interrogated by the Gestapo, when McGillvary's dog tags were discovered in his pocket.

The Germans threatened them with being shot as spies unless they told them all the details of their journey from the time of being shot down. However none would talk except to give their Name, Rank and Serial Numbers as required as POW's. Each of them were interrogated several times an than taken to the Prison de St. Gilles and thrown into dark, filthy cells. .

While no physical harm was experiences by the POW;s, McGillvary recalled seeing civilians that had been badly beaten, one elderly woman in particular with badly bruised legs from being repeatedly being kicked during interrogation. In a another instance a man had his teeth pulled out for refusing to answer questions.

On September 2, 1944 The POW's were than to be transported in Boxcars by Train to a prisoner of war camps and the political prisoners to no doubt concentration or work camps. And who knows, that might have been the end of the story for all of them if not for the heroic efforts of the Dutch Resistance.

In what has been described as "The Ghost Train", After the train left the station in Brussels it ventured only a few miles, when it was ordered back to the rail yard because the railroad tracks had been destroyed. In the next couple of days the coordinated efforts of the resistance and railroad workers lead to release of the political prisoners and the train eventually being derailed outside of Brussels on September 4th. The train and POW's were abandoned by the German troops.

McGillvary and the POW;s were able to break free from the Boxcars and made their way tin groups of Two and Three towards Allied lines near the village of Schaerbeek where they made contact with Canadian troops.

Chapter 9

After the War for Casey and the Crew of the *Aliquippa*

After returning to the United States, Casey Paulinski remained in the Army Air Corps, attending personnel affairs school in New York City and then administrative school in Boulder, Colorado. He was honorably discharged from active duty with the rank of first lieutenant at Randolph Field in Texas on January 15, 1947. During his service he received three Bronze Stars, an American Theater Campaign Medal, and a Victory Medal. He remained in the air force reserves, reaching the rank of Captain.

Once back in Chicago, Casey went to work for the Ford Motor Company at its aircraft engine plant on the southwest side of the city. There he used his aeronautics expertise to test jet engines. The site would later become the location of Chicago's first shopping mall, appropriately named Ford City.

Casey started dating Leanore Serepuk, a young girl who lived in the same two flat apartment building her family owned on Harding Avenue where Casey and his family also lived. The two married on January 12, 1951. Leaving Ford, Casey went to work at a Nabisco Company Bakery and later was a bus driver for the Chicago Transit Authority. He also enjoyed being an active member of the Knights of Columbus. Casey and Lennie, as she was affectionately called, raised three daughters and a son—Linda, Diane, Juanita, and James.

The war and the POW experience took its toll on Casey. What we now know as post-traumatic stress syndrome wasn't as widely understood or as readily treated years ago. In addition, many veterans were hesitant to seek psychiatric treatment, fearing that if an employer found out they were "seeing a shrink" they could be out of work.

"My dad didn't sleep well due to nightmares and didn't like the sound of train horns and the sound of rail cars uncoupling," Diane said. "My mom told me that he didn't handle being woken up abruptly, due to his prisoner of war memories."

Casey also suffered pain from frostbite in his toes and later developed lung and throat cancer. His battle with cancer would continue for nine years, taking an emotional, social, and financial toll on Casey and his family. He underwent experimental cobalt and radiation cancer treatments, which at times required him to keep a minimum distance of ten feet from his young children. This was confusing for all family members to witness and equally difficult to explain to them.

As the cancer spread from his throat to his stomach, Casey required a tracheotomy and a feeding tube. "I remember at the age of twelve or thirteen having to suction out his trach when he was too weak to do it himself," said Diane. "Maybe that's one of the reasons I later on became a registered nurse.

"My memories of my dad are also filled with many happy times," she said. "I fondly remember pool parties in our backyard with all the neighborhood children. My parents set up a cardboard grocery store and helped us give out hot dogs, potato chips, and lemonade. Our family would sing songs and make a whirlpool effect in our swimming pool long into the summer nights."

Diane also fondly remembered extended family gatherings that spilled out into the backyard. The Paulinskis once had a neighbor take a picture of all twenty-five-plus relatives.

Near the end of Casey's life, in the winter of 1973, Lennie brought a miniature ceramic Christmas tree to his hospital room, where his family attempted to celebrate the holy season. Casey died on January 9, 1974, at fifty-four after a long and painful battle with cancer. Diane recalled that at her father's passing, her mother said, "Daddy is now at peace." Casey was buried at Resurrection Cemetery in Justice, a southwest suburb of Chicago on what would have been his twenty-third wedding anniversary.

Hank Roeber

After returning to Long Island, New York, and to his wife, Ruth, and their first child Marty, Hank Roeber went back to work with the Pennsylvania Railroad as a dining car steward. He later worked as a brakeman for the Long Island Rail Road before reenlisting for active service in the air force. Hank and Ruth would have two more boys, Tom and Robert.

Hank reported for duty in Great Falls, Montana, and was assigned to pilot C-47 transports. Under normal circumstances, he would have been preparing for the Berlin Airlift. However, because he had been a prisoner of war in Germany, he was prohibited from being sent for duty there. He was instead sent to Japan where he spent the next two years, beginning a long postwar military career that saw him based in faraway places like the Aleutian Islands and Tripoli, Libya. Hank also spent seven years flying C-47s, C-54s, and C131s while based in San Antonio, Texas.

He served in the military for twenty-seven years, winding up at Scott Air Force Base in southern Illinois. Hank and his family settled in the town of New Baden. He retired with the rank of lieutenant colonel. For a number of years he stayed active as a pilot, flying executive jets for Remmit-Warner, and also worked ground control at Scott Air Force Base.

Hank always retained his love of trains and acquired an impressive collection of model trains that he proudly displayed in his home. He was also adept at woodworking and remained active in veterans affairs as a member of the American Legion.

Hank Roeber passed away at eighty-nine on January 13, 2009, at a hospital in Belleville, Illinois, and is buried along with his beloved wife, Ruth, at Greenmount Cemetery in New Baden, Illinois. Ruth died in November of 2009 at ninety-two.

Donald McPhee

Little is known about Don McPhee after the war, but I learned that he was a registered civil engineer and self-employed contractor. His wife's name was Beth. He continued to live in California, eventually moving about two hundred miles south to Templeton where he died on November 26, 1979, three days shy of his 60th birthday. He had at least one sibling, a sister, Patricia Roberts, who at the time of his death lived somewhere in Virginia.

Seymour Wolfson

After the war Seymour married Rosalyn Lissauer in 1951 and adopted two brothers, Thomas and Clifford. He went. in to the home remodeling business in the Akron area and earned the nickname "Tin Man" for his work installing among other items aluminum siding. He rarely talked about his experiences during the war, especially his time as a prisoner of war. He died on November 28, 2000 at the age of 85. He left a legacy of Six grandchildren.

Clayton Verlo.

Clayton and his wife Lillian and their three children, Patty, Karen and Allen lived in the Chicago area in the suburb of Des Plaines for many years after the war and worked for the Richardson Company in the western suburb of Melrose Park, manufacturers of asphalt shingles, roll roofing, and composition battery casing. In 1984 when Clayton retired he and his wife moved to his hometown of LaCrosse, Wisconsin.

After suffering a Stroke in 1998 he moved into a Veterans Administration Hospital and then eventually moved with his wife to Virginia to be closer to his oldest daughter Pat. Clayton passed away on February 1, 2011 in Virginia at the age of 89. Besides his two daughters and Son, he leaves behind a legacy of Six grandchildren and as of 2011, seven great grandchildren

Royce McGillvary

After returning to America, Royce McGillvary would eventually make his way to the west coast and Los Angeles where he would work for many years with both Bethlehem and United States Steel, He would pass away on July 28, 2001 at the age of 88

Irvin Sumpter

After being liberated from Stalag 13D at Moosburg by General George Patton's 3rd Army on April 29th, 1945, he returned to the states on June 23rd and in August married Blanche Hawkins. He continued in the Air Force and completed a 21-year career as a flight engineer, jet engine aircraft technician and aircraft maintenance supervisor retiring with the rank of Senior Master Sergeant.

For the next 21 years he would work for the Phillips Petroleum Company as a plastics technician in research and development. He even had a few patents to his name in the area of Plastics Blow Moulding. After retirement he engaged in farming, particularly enjoying caring for his Horses and Cattle. He was active in the Tulsa Chapter of the Ex-Prisoners of War. Irvin Died on May 19, 1997 in Bartlesville, Oklahoma at the age of 74

Hubert O'Neill

Hubert worked for the Federal Government for 37 years as an engineer technician, working at the Watertown and Piscataway, New Jersey Arsenals. He married Marry Elizabeth "Betty" Farrell in 1951 and they had a son Dennis. Hubert and Betty eventually moved back to Massachusetts on Cape Cod. He was a commander of a VFW post, and a member of the Knights of Columbus. He passed away on February 27, 2004 at the age of 79.

Walter Sybo

After returning stateside in June of 45' and leaving active service in the military in late October, Walt married Anna Maria Costanzo in January of 1946. Sadly Water's Father, Stanley would die in May of that year at the age of 49.

He went into the Auto Sales business and was quite successful, selling at various times everything from Chryslers, Fords and even DeSotos. Walt and Anna had one child, a daughter Sharryn who was born in 1947. He passed away on October 27, 2003 at the age of 79.

George Sokolsky (Kols)

George Sokolsky retuned to America and his Wife, Evelyn and was discharged in November of 1945. He worked for the Rochester Telephone Company for 30+ years as an Engineer and Manager. Sokolsky had a brother Robert, who also worked for Rochester Telephone, and to avoid confusion and make a name for himself, he legally changed his last name to Kols. The couple had one daughter, Charlene and after she graduated from college in 1969 the family moved to Florida where George continued work as a contractor for various telephone companies. After George's Wife Evelyn passed away in 1999, after 57 Years of Marriage, he moved to Southern California to be closer to his daughter and her husband Jim Kilroy. George Sokolsky Kols died on October 19, 2004, five days after his 88th birthday.

Casey with his nephew Dennis Paulinski at Chicago's Midway Airport

Casey and family members: (L-R) Mother Eleanor, Brother in Law Ed
Dryjan, Sister Joanne Paulinski Dryjan, Nieces Virgie and Little Bernadette

Casey and Lennie's Wedding Photo, 1951

Casey, baby Linda and Lennie

Casey and Lennie with their four children, Linda, Nini, Diane and
Jamie enjoying their backyard swimming pool in Chicago.

Nini and Diane celebrate with their brother Jamie at his Eagle Scout Ceremony

The Paulinski Family Celebrate Diane & Mark's Wedding.
L-R) Granddaughter Teresa Kedzuf, Nini Paulinski, Granddaughter
Samantha Paulinski, Linda Paulinski Snesrud, Diane & Mark, Lennie
Paulinski, Granddaughter Lisa Kedzuf and Grandson Johnny Kedzuf

Paulinski Sisters, Linda, Diane & Nini

Six of the Crew reunite at Wright-Patterson Air Force Base in Dayton, Ohio
(L-R) Walter Sybo, George Sokosky Kols , Clayton Verlo,
Hubert O'Neill, Irvin Sumpter and Hank Roeber

Diane, Mark & Louis with Ruth and Hank Roeber at a local
restaurant in their hometown of New Baden, Illinois

Mark and Diane visiting with Betty and Hubert O'Neill at
a restaurant near their home on Cape Cod, MA.

Mark at reunion he organized with George Sokolsky
Kols and Royce McGillvary in Los Angeles

Lennie, Diane, Louis and Mark next to a B-17, the first time Lennie had seen the aircraft her Husband Casey had flown in World War II

Til Kenkhuis with Children's Dress made with material
from World War II Allied Airman's Parachute

Mark and Pietertje with can of coffee Casey sent her family as thank you gift in October, 1945. It was saved but never opened by the family.

Casey's Great Grandsons, Colton & Ezra

The Farina-Paulinski Family, Diane, Louis, Mark and Bella.

Chapter 10

The Journey to Discovery

One day in early January 2002 I was doing a people search on Yahoo to see what would pop up about me and other family members on Internet sites. I knew that a well-known club disc jockey from Chicago named Mark Farina had a website. In fact, for a number of years people would ask me if I was doing DJ work on the side, because they had seen my name on some dance club marquee in Chicago.

I found a number of sites with either a photo credit or a quote from my work as a public relations representative with the Chicago Department of Environment, and I saw links to stories I had written for the prep sports section of the *Chicago Sun-Times*. I also typed in my dad's name because he had been a Chicago alderman.

I am still not sure why I did this, but something made me type in my father-in-law's name, Casimir Paulinski. Immediately two web links appeared—a list of POWs from World War II and a much more detailed site dedicated to the POWs of Stalag Luft 1. On this site, www.merkki. com, Casimir Paulinski was listed as a second lieutenant from Illinois housed in the south compound.

I was astonished to have found this information about a man whom I had never met and who had been deceased for twenty-eight years. I excitedly asked my wife to look at the family artifacts from World War II and tell me what camp her father had been in. Indeed it was Stalag Luft 1, and I told her what I had found on the Internet. She was as stunned as

I was and examined the website, which had been created by Mary Freer and Barbara Smith, the daughters of Dick Williams, an American airmen who had been a POW at this camp.

It is an amazing site, one of the most informative historical websites I have ever encountered. Mary and Barbara have provided many details about the camp, including information about the commandants and the number of guards. They have even come up with a partial list of POW roommates.

Armed with a clearer picture of the POW camp and using the web links supplied by the site, I started to wonder what had happened to the rest of Casey's crew. Did they all survive the downing of the plane? What had happened to them after the war, and did any keep in contact with Casey?

The questions far outnumbered the answers, and the first question was, what were the crewmen's names? We knew from Casey's discharge papers that he had been in the Eighth Air Force's Ninety-Second Bomb Group and had been shot down on December 22, 1943. The next step was to reach out to the Eighth Air Force Museum in Savannah, Georgia, to request information on the crew.

The Stalag Luft 1 website provided a link to the museum site, and I sent an e-mail to the museum historian for help. Within two days I received a list of the names of the crew members as well their hometowns in 1943. In addition, through the website Heavybombers.com, I found a link to the Ninety-Second Bomb Group historical organization. The group's historian, retired Col. Robert Elliott, sent me a copy of the missing-air-crew report from December 22, 1943.

Though its negative aspects are widely known, the Internet is a remarkable resource for research, saving the time and effort of traveling to a library. This is not to say that libraries are not an equally excellent source of materials, especially for those who do not have a home computer or access to the Internet. I made extensive use of this time-tested resource. I also used Yahoo's white pages feature, a nationwide phone book on the Internet.

The first person I found by using this tool was Walt Sybo. In the first week of January 2002 I dialed the number in Sewickley, Pennsylvania, and spoke to his wife Josephine. She was amazed to learn the answer to what had been a mystery to Walt and to members of the crew: what had happened to Casey Paulinski after the war?

Walt had stayed close to his hometown of Pittsburgh. Sadly I was not able to talk to him, because he was in a Veterans Administration hospital after suffering a series of strokes.

Josephine, or Jo as she called herself, wrote to us a few days later and said that when she had visited the hospital and had told Walt about the phone call with me, a tear had run down his face. He was saddened to learn that Casey had died twenty-eight years earlier, but he had finally gotten closure about what had happened to his friend.

Walt had always spoken highly of Casey, respecting him as a pilot and appreciating his friendship. Operating in close quarters, standing directly behind the cockpit, Walt would have gotten to know Casey well. Their shared Polish-American heritage may also have helped create a friendship.

Jo told us that she and Walt had traveled to the Netherlands in 1984 with other crew members to celebrate the fortieth anniversary of the liberation of Holland by Allied troops and that they had continued to correspond with their friends in Europe. Among them was a daughter of the couple who had sheltered Casey, Hank, and Walt after they had belly-landed the crippled B-17.

The book *In Verdrukking, Verzet en Vrijheid*, about the war in Holland, included a couple of chapters about the crew. Jo was gracious enough to mail us a copy of those chapters and the cover of the book. Diane and I were stunned to see a picture of a young Casey that he had sent to the family after the war. The discovery left Diane nearly speechless and overcome with emotion.

About the time I was tracking down Walt Sybo, I struck gold by finding the phone number of Hubert O'Neill in Massachusetts. I immediately called him. It was the first of many telephone conversations with Hubert and his lovely wife Betty as well as countless e-mails between us. Hubert said Hank Roeber was alive and well in southern Illinois, and this news led to a memorable call to Hank and Ruth.

Hubert, Hank, and others I later contacted all talked about the fun-loving Casey and how much they liked and respected him. If only I could have shared this with Casey and Lennie. In a unique way I think I was communicating with them in some spiritual way. In fact, in an e-mail just a few days after our initial phone conversation, Hubert O'Neill wrote, "It was almost like hearing a voice from the past." Hubert also mentioned that Casey had always wanted to be a P-38 fighter pilot rather than a bomber copilot.

When I had worked in sales, if I got a quick sale early in the day I was motivated to pursue the next one. The same held true for my research about the crew. My success in finding members of the crew and gaining detailed information drove me to keep searching and learning more about the air war and the bombers that flew over Europe. My appetite for information was insatiable. I perused the history sections of bookstores and libraries and looked up websites related to B-17s, POW camps, and the Eighth Air Force. I also picked up numerous copies of World War II history periodicals.

I have always been fascinated with history, particularly American history, so this research was right up my alley. I had known little about the air war in Europe and even less about the particulars of the aircraft used to fight the battles. Four years later my knowledge has grown considerably, and what were simple facts now have a more significant meaning. For anyone looking to learn about this period in world history, I highly recommend the works of Roger A. Freeman, who is considered the preeminent historian of the Eighth Air Force. Gerald Astor is also a terrific resource and has written a number of books about the war including one about the Eighth Air Force.

With my newfound information, I continued to try to contact the other crewmen and their families. Two men in particular presented a challenge: Donald McPhee and Royce McGillvary. McPhee's whereabouts were unknown to six of the crewmen who had gotten together for a reunion, and McGillvary was a mystery. Irvin Sumpter was the only crew member who knew much about him, and he had died by the time I started my research.

Again the Internet was a great resource. I was perusing the website Geneaology.com and came across the Social Security Death Index. We knew from Casey's artifacts that McPhee had lived somewhere near San Francisco, California, during the war. On a hunch, based on an estimate of how old Donald McPhee would have been in 1943, I looked under his name in the index and narrowed my search down to two entries in California. I then dialed directory assistance in Templeton, California, and struck gold.

It turned out that Donald's wife, Beth, who had recently passed away, had kept the telephone listing in her husband's name even though he had died twenty-three years earlier. Beth's niece, Patricia Townsend Pratt, was now living in the house and told me as much as she could about her aunt and uncle. She sent me proof sheets of photos from Stalag Luft 1, some of which I had seen on other websites. However, we lost contact shortly after, and I was still left with questions.

I knew through the Social Security Death Index that Donald had died in November 1979 in Templeton, but I knew little about his vocation in life. I eventually called the public library in neighboring San Luis Obispo and asked that staff research obituaries from November 1979 to find a Donald McPhee. Shortly after making this request in writing, I received a copy of Don McPhee's obituary, which had appeared in the *San Luis Obispo Telegraph-Tribune*. The article shed light on his life before and after the war.

With the help of Jo Sybo and Betty O'Neill, I secured telephone numbers and addresses for Clayton Verlo and Irvin Sumpter. Those initial phone calls were equally memorable experiences. Clayton Verlo, like Walt Sybo, was in a VA hospital, but I was able to talk and correspond with his wife, Lillian.

Blanche Sumpter was also very helpful, telling me about her husband's life before and after the war. She sent me a brief biography of Irvin and a copy of his formal military photo from the war.

But simply talking on the telephone wasn't enough. We had to make the trek to meet some of these people who had been part of a crucial period in Casey's life. Diane had known about them only from a crew photo, and they could shed light on the person that her father was during the war. Meeting each other would also offer closure for Diane and for the crew members. This would take a while since we were attempting to place Lennie Paulinski's property and estate in order.

Meeting the Pilot and the Radio Operator

We boarded an Amtrak train at Chicago's Union Station to take us to St. Louis for our meeting with Hank and Ruth Roeber. The trip was also exciting since it was our son's first long train ride. We had taken short commuter rides on Chicago's Metra, but we would travel six hours to meet a person who had played an important role in shaping Casey Paulinski's life.

After arriving at the train depot in St. Louis (at the time a surprisingly isolated, dreary, and cramped little facility for a great city), we rode a taxi to the car rental office and then made our way to the Roebers' home. The ride took us across the Mississippi River into Illinois and the small town of New Baden.

Hank and Ruth had settled in New Baden because of its close proximity to Scott Air Force Base where Hank was stationed before retiring from the military. To say that Diane and I were excited about finally meeting Hank would be a tremendous understatement.

After we had visited for a while with the Roebers, I set up my camcorder and interviewed Hank. It was like stepping back in time as he recounted the crew's early days and the details about being shot down on that fateful day in December '43.

Diane thanked Hank for his part in "saving the world" and for safely landing the aircraft and making her dad's eventual return home possible. It was an emotional moment for her, one we will always remember. Hank and Ruth then took us to a local restaurant where we continued to share stories, Diane about her family, and Hank and Ruth about their family and their life together. We will always cherish this wonderful experience.

The second trip we made was to the East Coast to meet Hubert and Betty O'Neill in Cape Cod. Our trek in August of 2002 began with a stop in Baltimore, Maryland, to see Diane's new neurologist at Johns Hopkins University Hospital. Diane had recently been diagnosed with a rare condition called transverse myelitis, an autoimmune neurological disorder, which among other symptoms significantly affects the strength and mobility of her legs. Unfortunately, this disease, like many other lesser-known disorders, doesn't get the publicity or the research funding that go to the related multiple sclerosis.

We spent about twenty-four hours in Baltimore, visiting doctors at Johns Hopkins and seeing the city. Highlights included a wonderful dinner at Phillips Restaurant in the Inner Harbor and tours of the Civil War ship the *USS Constellation* and Oriole Park at Camden Yards. The next day we flew to Boston.

Arriving in Boston that afternoon, we ventured into the historic North End for a lovely dinner at one of the many fabulous Italian restaurants. The next day I toured historic Fenway Park. Baseball players were going to strike that day unless they and the club owners could come to a last-minute agreement. The Red Sox were in their clubhouse, waiting to see if they would board a bus for a road trip or go home. Fortunately, while we were touring the park, an agreement on a tentative contract was announced. It was a terrific experience to walk out onto the gravel in this baseball shrine and to take pictures next to the scoreboard and the famous Green Monster in left field.

We rented a car and made our way to Cape Cod. With great anticipation, we arrived at the home of Hubert and Betty O'Neill and were warmly greeted by this wonderful couple. After getting to know each other and sharing refreshments, I again set up my videocam and recorded Hubert's memories of the war and especially about Casey and the crew.

He spoke highly of Casey and shared a few of the comical stories that I have mentioned in the book. Hubert was really only a kid when they were shot down, having just turned nineteen.

In our short but memorable time with Hubert and Betty, they gave us a tour of the Cape Cod sites. We saw a memorial to President John F. Kennedy and drove through some of the coastal towns. And of course, when in Cape Cod, it was only appropriate to eat fresh seafood at a popular restaurant. We spent the night as guests of the O'Neill's in a room provided by their condo association. Hubert said he never would have imagined that some sixty years later he would be sitting with Casey's daughter.

I wish we could have spent more time with the O'Neill's and the Roebers, but our short time together was memorable. The experience was somewhat bittersweet for Diane, because she couldn't share all of this with her parents. However, she did get answers to many questions she had had about her father's experiences in the war.

Another avenue I explored was to reach out to the local newspaper in the Aliquippa, Pennsylvania area to find out why their B-17 aircraft that the crew was flying in had been called USS Aliquippa, a designation afforded that of a ship.

I contacted Gino Piroli, a columnist for the Beaver County Times & Allegheny Times who interviewed me and beginning in June of 2004 wrote a series of columns asking people in the area if anyone knew why the B-17 had this unusual name.

The best theory is that a local steel manufacturing plant had participated in a number of War Bond drives, to raise money for needed military items like ships, aircraft, etc. Maybe they hadn't raised enough funds for a warship and instead designated it towards an aircraft.

Chapter 11

A Reunion of the Bombardier and the Missing Waist Gunner

Royce McGillvary was the replacement waist gunner for that fateful mission in 1943. Because they hadn't met him until boarding the B-17 that day, the crew members didn't really know him. What had happened to him was a mystery, but again through the Internet, I quickly located him in Los Angeles.

When I first called, Royce was astonished that I had found him and appreciative that I hadn't forgotten him. The one crew member he had gotten to know was Irvin Sumpter, and that was under the most of unusual circumstances as they evaded capture for a few weeks after bailing out of the crippled plane.

Coincidentally, bombardier George Sokolsky had recently moved to Southern California to live with his daughter and her family. This presented an exciting opportunity to reunite these two men.

In April of 2004, I arranged for a meeting of these two gentlemen at the Westin Hotel near Los Angeles International Airport. After taking a late flight from Chicago and checking in at the hotel around midnight, I had a restless night anticipating the reunion of these two men after sixty years. I had arranged with the hotel to reserve a small meeting room and to have refreshments available.

That morning I was beyond excited about what was to occur. It is difficult to put into words my emotions, but suffice it to say the event was bigger than I was. One question occurred to me: would I recognize them when they arrived? I had never seen a photo of Royce McGillvary, and I didn't know what George Sokolsky looked like except for a couple of photos taken in 1943 before he embarked on his trip overseas.

The first to arrive was George along with his daughter Charlene and son-in-law Jim Kilroy. I immediately sensed it was George, and we all warmly greeted each other. After waiting a few minutes, we made our way to the meeting room and got better acquainted. Shortly after, Royce walked in, and he and George greeted each other. Watching them share stories and compare notes after sixty years was like taking a trip back in time and viewing history from the sidelines. It was as if they were young men and were getting up to speed. Again I set up my video camera and recorded the two comparing notes and sharing experiences.

The moment became all the more poignant when Charlene informed me that her father had been diagnosed with terminal cancer. It turned out he had only six months more to live.

This was a memorable morning, and I felt as if I was performing an important service for all veterans and their families, not just George and Royce. It was an honor and an experience I will never forget.

I took advantage of my short time in Southern California, attending a baseball game at Dodger Stadium and venturing to Hollywood as a tourist and visiting the Wax Museum and the Hollywood Walk of Fame. This twenty-four-hour whirlwind was one of the most memorable experiences I have ever had.

Chapter 12

Casey's Fellow Pilot from Chicago

Art Pinzke was in many ways a mirror image of Casey, coming from Chicago and taking an eerily similar path in the war. Finding him and getting to know him proved invaluable, allowing me to learn about the experiences they shared in pilot training.

Among the mementos that my mother-in-law Lennie saved from Casey's war years were two yearbooks that he had received during his pilot training days at Victory Field in Vernon, Texas, and at Frederick Air Field in Oklahoma. These books chronicled the goings-on at the airfields, much like a high school yearbook chronicles the activities of a school and its students.

Pouring over the information in the book from Victory Field, I found that one other cadet besides Casey was from Chicago. Locating Art Pinzke wasn't difficult because he had remained in the Chicago area after the war and was in the phone book. One night I telephoned him and introduced myself. I will never forget Art's reaction. "Casey—he got shot down on his fifth or sixth mission." It seemed like this had happened yesterday and not sixty years ago, and Art remembered without hesitation. Even more amazing was that they had been assigned to the same squadron in England, had both been B-17 copilots, had been shot down months apart, and had wound up in the same POW camp.

Art's detailed memories of the two men training together were important, filling a gap that existed because we had found nothing written by Casey about this important period. In many ways talking to Art was like talking to Casey. After a closer look at the scrapbook that Casey's sister Joanne had compiled during the war, I realized that Art and Casey's families had kept in contact while the boys were away, and in letters home from the POW camp, Casey mentioned Art's arrival.

Joanne had also collected articles from Chicago papers reporting that Art was missing in action and then had become a POW. Besides talking with him numerous times on the phone, I visited with Art and videotaped his recollections from the war years.

Art had stayed independent after the passing of his wife, and until a fall that broke his hip, he remained in a comfortable apartment in the Chicago suburb of Des Plaines until moving into a veterans hospital in the suburb of North Chicago. He Died on August 18, 2011 at the age of 95.

Chapter 13

Our Friends in the Netherlands

When I first communicated with a member of the crew's family, Jo Sybo, I learned about the role that townspeople in Holland had played in sheltering three crewmen, putting themselves in great danger by doing so. Most amazing to me, especially considering the limited means of communication available immediately after the war, was how people from across the ocean in Europe were able to track down Casey Paulinski in the United States. But that is precisely what they did, and in October of 1945 Casey wrote a letter back to Pietertje Pieters, the teenage daughter of the family that heroically aided Casey, Hank, and Walt.

"I am indeed very happy and grateful to you for writing to me," Casey wrote. "While I was in France, I thought of visiting you people, but my time did not permit me to do so. However, I never expected to hear from you. Thank you for your thoughtfulness." He ended the two-page handwritten note by saying, "I want to thank you and your family for all you have done for me."

Casey also sent a thank-you gift, a can of Thomas J. Webb coffee from his hometown of Chicago.

Hubert O'Neill, Walt Sybo, and Irvin Sumpter visited Holland in 1984 as guests of the people of the Borne. They were treated like returning heroes and enjoyed a memorable few days, which included a parade and banquets. One of the surprises was a float carrying a replica of the *USS Aliquippa*.

Hubert and Betty helped us contact a friend they had made while in Holland, Til Kenkhuis, whose family had also sheltered downed Allied airmen. We first communicated by e-mail and then by a series of letters and finally by long-distance telephone. Til had been assisting Pietertje Pieters in trying to find Casey and his family all those years after their initial correspondence. They had never given up. In many ways, finding this missing link was as important to them as it was to us.

In our conversations and other correspondence it became apparent that more than sixty years later, the Dutch people had tremendous regard and appreciation for the Allied troops who had liberated their country.

Til Kenkhuis was an important conduit to the events of December 22, 1943, and to the people of Holland. She scanned onto a CD the thank-you letter and photo that Casey had sent to Pietertje's family as well as a photo of the can of coffee that he had sent as a gift, which the family had saved, unopened, for all those years. She also scanned thank-you letters from the governments of the United States, Great Britain, and the Netherlands acknowledging their contributions, at great risk to their families, in sheltering downed Allied airmen.

It was equally important that we had helped these people answer questions about three members of the crew whom they had long attempted to find. They now knew what had happened to Donald McPhee, Royce McGillvary, and Casey Paulinski. All this was again bittersweet for my wife, Diane, because as was the case with our conversations and visits with the Roebers and the O'Neill, she couldn't share the news with her parents.

In November of 2009 I made arrangements to travel to Europe to visit the Netherlands countryside where the *USS Aliquippa* had come down. With the frequent flier miles we had accumulated from our credit card use, I was able to afford the trip, which included side journeys to Paris, France, and to the country of my grandparents, Italy. As president of the Forest Glen-Mayfair Kiwanis Club in Chicago, I also reached out through the worldwide network of Kiwanis to visit fellow Kiwanians in the Dutch town of Almelo and in Rome.

I felt it was important to talk to people who had lived through the war and who may have been a part of this chapter in history. While a great deal of information can be gathered by phone and from the Internet and reference materials, nothing can replace traveling to a foreign land, soaking up the atmosphere, and meeting people face to face.

So on a Sunday afternoon in mid-November 2009, I boarded a United Airlines flight from Chicago, and after changing planes at Dulles Airport in Washington, DC, made the overnight trans-Atlantic journey to Amsterdam.

This was a first for me. The seven-hour flight left Washington at 7:00 p.m. and arrived the next morning in Amsterdam at ten. I spent the first day mostly as a tourist in a foreign country, checking out the Venice of Northern Europe. As expected for mid-November, it was rainy and around forty degrees.

A highlight was my visit to the Anne Frank House and Museum. In this building, the young girl and her family had hidden from the Nazis occupying the Netherlands. It was a sobering experience to walk the stairwells, the corridors, and the rooms that this frightened yet amazingly mature girl had written about in her incredible diary. I could only imagine what she and her family must have felt, and I couldn't conceive of the horrors they faced after being found out and sent to concentration camps. My heart ached for Anne and for the family members and friends who suffered and died at the hands of the Nazis. I grieved in particular for her father Otto, the only one in the family to survive their atrocities.

As the only passenger on this rainy day, I also took what wound up being a private canal boat tour, guided by a onetime foreign exchange student at Michigan State University. His perfect English and our common familiarity with the Midwest and one of his favorite cities, Chicago, made learning about Amsterdam and the Netherlands a delight.

Day two started out bright and early with a two-hour train trip from Centraal Station in Amsterdam to the eastern Dutch town of Almelo. The weather was much better than the day before. I arrived at the station under partly cloudy skies and was greeted by Til and Pietertje. We drove the short distance to the charming home of Til and her husband Gerhard in Bornebroek where we sat down over coffee and cookies and got reacquainted.

To say that my adrenaline was flowing would be a gross understatement. This visit was for me almost déjà vu, like when I had arranged for Royce McGillvary and George Sokolsky to meet for the first time in sixty years in

Los Angeles. I can only imagine the thoughts that were running through Til and Pietertje's minds as this stranger whom they knew only through a few photos, e-mails, and phone calls sat talking about his family in America and about familiar names from many years past.

Til brought out a white dress for a little girl and explained that her mother had sewn it from the parachute of one of the downed Allied airmen. She had mentioned this in a previous e-mail, but to see the dress was quite amazing. I felt I was viewing a museum piece without having to visit the museum.

We then made our way to the farm field where the aircraft had come down. As I visualized the huge Flying Fortress gliding overhead, I felt I was being transported back in time. The site reminded me of my grandfather Philip Farina's blueberry farm in New Buffalo, Michigan, because it was just a few hundred yards away from a modern expressway, which in the case of both farms, didn't exist sixty-five years ago. I could imagine how the bomber would have terrified a young Jan Bolscher as he was plowing the field.

We made our way to the site of Pietertje's old home where the crew members had sought refuge. She pointed out the railroad tracks and the path that the three men took as they walked, no doubt cold, hungry, and scared.

Pietertje's parents worked for the railroad, raising and lowering the gates as trains approached the crossing. They worked twelve-hour shifts six days a week. We were greeted at the empty parcel of land by two geese that now resided there and seemed to know their way around the fenced-in premises.

Pietertje said her parents had come close to being investigated when one of them forgot to lower the gates for an approaching train. If the engineer had reported this to his supervisors, the complaint would have brought unwanted visits by railroad officials, or worse. Thankfully the engineer said nothing, and her parents' work with the Dutch underground and the sheltering of downed Allied airmen were not discovered.

We then stopped for a pleasant lunch at a bakery and restaurant in the picture-postcard town of Bornebroek. Here and at countless other points I wished that Diane was with me. I was also reminded of just how commercialized and plastic so many parts of the United States have become. I didn't see any Walmarts, Costcos, Targets, or tacky strip malls while touring the Dutch countryside. I know stores like those exist in Europe, but it was delightful to experience an environment that recalled a simpler, less commercialized time. I was again reminded of the difference almost as soon as I got off the plane in Chicago and took the cab ride back home.

After lunch we drove to Pietertje's home in Dipenheim where I set up my digital video camera and interviewed Til and Pietertje. While we were talking, Pietertje pulled out mementos from many years ago—the letter from Casey to her, the can of coffee, newspaper clippings, and family photos.

Our adrenaline rose and our emotions flowed. I had to share the moment with Diane, so I called her on my cell phone. It was about 9:00 a.m. Chicago time when I reached her and shared what was happening a few thousand miles away. Diane was overwhelmed by emotion and started to cry. I handed the phone to Pietertje, and Diane thanked her for all that her family had done for Casey. Then she said something that I know she truly felt: "We love you!"

When I asked Pietertje about the penalty for harboring enemy soldiers, she pointed her finger like a gun and said they all would have been immediately shot by the Germans. So why did they risk their lives for strangers? Her simple but powerful response was that it was the right thing to do for those risking their lives to liberate them.

The risk these people took was enormous, and yet they acted with little hesitation. They were suffering all the hardships of the war: severe food shortages, forced labor, lack of freedom, and an incomprehensible cruelty that many in our world today seem to forget.

I looked at Pietertje and suddenly saw not an old lady but a young woman of nineteen with dreams that were being threatened by militaristic neighbors from across the border. These people didn't appear at first glance to be any different from her neighbors and friends in Goor, but she certainly realized that they were not her friends and that one false move meant a cruel imprisonment or even death.

Our interview was cut short because we had an important appointment with Dutch author and village historian Henne Nordhuis at the Borne town hall. This is a beautiful modern facility with a charming cafeteria for employees and visitors. We sat down with Henne over tea and cookies and shared our research. Henne said the local people had looked for Casey for the fortieth anniversary celebration of the end of World War II in the Netherlands but had discovered that he had died. We exchanged gifts. I gave the three of them souvenir books about Chicago, and Til and Pietertje gave me silver coins from the Netherlands to share with Diane and her sisters. Henne gave me a collection of photos from his archives that had been taken shortly after the *Aliquippa* had belly-landed in the farm field. We exchanged business cards and promised to keep in touch.

That evening Til, Pietertje, and I shared a wonderful dinner at a beautiful hotel restaurant in Goor, capping off a day that I believe none of us will forget. After dinner, they drove me back to the train station in Almelo, and we said our good-byes. On the train ride back to Amsterdam that night, I felt a range of emotions and wished to return as soon as possible to this wonderful land, the next time with Diane and Louis.

The next morning I boarded a bullet train from Amsterdam to Paris and was fortunate to sit next to a friendly and helpful gentleman from Paris who suggested important stops to make during my seven-hour layover in the City of Lights. The announcements on the train were made in four languages—French, Dutch, German, and English. This is something for Americans to consider. We are quick to criticize bilingual signs and announcements in our country when we have Mexico, a Spanish-speaking country, as our neighbor to the south. The practice in Europe gave me a different perspective on this subject and reminded me just how much of a melting pot our country is and why that makes it such a unique and wonderful place. The Europeans don't seem to complain about multiple languages, so why should we?

While in Paris I took a quick taxi ride to the Cathedral of Notre Dame and to the Eiffel Tower. The cab drivers in Paris were particularly friendly and helpful to this stranger from America. It was amusing to see all the soccer fans from Ireland, dressed in colorful outfits, who were in town for a World Cup qualifying match with France. The cathedral was awe-inspiring and breathtaking. The Eiffel Tower was equally spectacular, just as I had always imagined it would be. I also stopped to watch the ships along the Seine River. To my surprise, though I was thousands of miles from home in a foreign country, I met fellow Chicagoans at the train station and shared a cup of coffee with them at a café while waiting to board the overnight train to Rome.

The train ride to Rome was an interesting experience as I shared a roomette with three other men. One was a middle-aged university professor from the north of France, another a young computer expert from Tuscany, and the third a retired chemical engineer from Rome. Fortunately there was no language barrier as they all spoke good English, and we spent much of the early evening comparing notes about our countries. The food, however, was very disappointing, and the accommodations on this older train were spartan, to say the least. I won't complain about Amtrak after this experience.

Rome was an absolute dream come true for this grandchild of Sicilian immigrants. To say I fell in love with Rome from the moment I stepped off the train the next morning would be a gross understatement. My accommodations at the Hotel Artemide on Via Nazionale were wonderful, the weather was magnificent—a balmy seventy-five degrees—and the sights were to die for. Seeing the Coliseum and the Roman Forum was another dream come true. I took the obligatory tourist photos with men dressed as Roman gladiators and felt like a kid in a candy shop.

Another memorable part of my trip to Rome was meeting and sharing dinner with a fellow member of Kiwanis International, Carmelo Cutuli, who graciously played tour guide, taking me to the Italian Parliament, the Pantheon, and the Trevi Fountain. The next night I attended a dinner meeting of the Roma Tevere Kiwanis Club and was welcomed by its president, Giancarlo Mancuso, at a wonderful ristorante and pizzeria, Il Barroccio, located on Via dei Pastini, around the corner from the Pantheon and the Trevi Fountain.

I received unexpected gifts in perfect weather and enjoyable, on-time flights from Washington, DC, to Amsterdam and back home from Rome to Philadelphia and on to Chicago.

I drift back often in my dreams to that trip. I was humbled to visit with people who had experienced war firsthand. We in America were spared such bloodshed for a long time. One of the lessons of 9-11 is that terrorism is not only a foreign phenomenon but a threat that we all must now be aware of, especially in major cities like New York and my hometown of Chicago.

Epilogue

On August 7, 2004, a beautiful summer Saturday, Diane, Louis, and I ventured back to Palwaukee Airport in Wheeling, Illinois, to see vintage World War II aircraft. The Collings Foundation had flown in a trio of its heavy bombers—a B-24 Liberator, a B-25 Mitchell, and a B-17 Flying Fortress, the *Nine-0-Nine*.

It had been almost three years since we had seen the Commemorative Air Force's B-17, the *Sentimental Journey*. This time Diane's mom Lennie was not with us. After climbing into and looking around the B-24 with Louis, I enjoyed the unique experience of being a passenger in a B-17.

Ten passengers and a crew of three traveled east along the Lake Michigan shoreline to downtown Chicago and back on the forty-minute flight. The trip was exhilarating. Of course the circumstances were dramatically different from those faced by the brave crews that flew in these planes during World War II. With temperatures in the low eighties at about 2,500 feet, we were able to wear summer shorts, short-sleeve shirts, and gym shoes.

A crew member would have worn a thick woolen flight suit and a parachute harness, totaling about fifty pounds, and would have flown in temperatures as low as forty degrees below zero. Add to this being in a cramped, unpressurized aircraft at altitudes of twenty thousand-plus feet and having to wear an uncomfortable oxygen mask.

To top things off, crewmen endured all this while bouncing from turbulence and antiaircraft flak and fending off enemy fighter planes shooting at them.

On the way back to Palwaukee Airport, I thought of all those young men who never returned home and of those who, like the crew of the *Aliquippa*, spent months and even years in the living hell of POW camps. This was a sobering thought and a deeply humbling one.

As I sat in the radio operator's seat that Hubert O'Neill had manned on the B-17, I thought of him and of Casey, Don, Walt, Sy, and Irvin, who were no longer with us but whose spirits and memories lived on with their families and their friends and very much with me.

Sadly, time and age took its toll on the crew members. When I started out on this journey of discovery, only four were deceased. However, when I finally completed this book, all ten had passed, and most of their spouses had gone to join them. Diane and I experienced emotional days when we found out about their passing, sometimes a year or more after the fact. Life marches on, and we are so distracted by our day-to-day activities that we can't always keep in touch as much as we would like.

I have grown to appreciate all the volunteers and aviation enthusiasts who have spent countless hours restoring the few remaining World War II aircraft to flying shape and taking these planes around the country to be seen by thousands of people of all ages.

My generation, the baby boomers born after World War II, now has the rare opportunity to see these aircraft up close and for a few dollars can experience, if only for a brief time, the feeling of flying in a vintage World War II airplane.

For some, like myself, there is a family connection; a parent, an in-law, or another relative flew these majestic birds. The experience has given me a kinship with these brave young men, in many cases just out of high school, the same age as my nephew Michael.

War is an awful tragedy. This book is in no way intended to glorify war or to minimize the devastating effects that each conflict has had not only upon the soldiers but upon countless innocent victims.

When militaristic regimes like the Nazis, Imperial Japan, and Fascist Italy or radical Muslim groups like ISIS and al Qaeda show a total disregard for human life, brave men and women must sacrifice to guarantee the freedoms of those who cannot defend themselves.

This is precisely what the United States and the other Allied countries did to rid the world of these regimes in World War II. The children and grandchildren of those brave soldiers and future generations owe an incredible debt of gratitude to those who sacrificed their lives and their innocence on the battlefields and in the skies of the South Pacific, North Africa, Europe, Asia, and India so that today we can live in freedom.

It is also important to acknowledge the efforts of all the people back in the United States who supplied the armed forces with the equipment and the supplies necessary to win the war. Countless women were thrust into the workforce and took up the heavy manual labor and other duties that men would have done if they hadn't been called to arms. These women—personified by Rosie the Riveter—played a significant role in the industrial juggernaut that turned the tide of the war in Europe and in the Pacific.

The American soldiers involved in the conflicts in Iraq and Afghanistan are sacrificing themselves for many of the same reasons that motivated those who served in World War II, and we owe them a debt of gratitude. While there has been a great debate over the justification for our involvement in those conflicts, I feel strongly that it is important to support our troops, even if many question the actions of our government and military leaders.

The men and women who have volunteered for military service are in the same age group as the men spotlighted in this book were when they went to war. While we may debate the justification, politics, and tactics of the Iraq and Afghanistan conflicts, particularly when families have lost loved ones, let's remember that what today's military people are doing for our country and for the world is much like what those brave young men did more than sixty years ago over the skies of Europe.

Acknowledgments

Where does one begin after taking such a fascinating and emotional journey over the past decade? I have read so many magazine articles and books and seen so many movies and documentaries about the air battles over Europe during World War II that it is almost impossible to say which influenced and educated me the most about the subject.

As a famous song from the World War II-related Musical *The Sound of Music* suggests, it's best to start at the very beginning. Certain works have been immensely helpful. These include *Citizen Soldier* and *The Wild Blue* by Stephen Ambrose, *The Mighty Eighth: The Air War in Europe as Told by the Men Who Fought It* by Gerald Astor, and the extensive documentation of the Eighth Air Force by official historian Roger A. Freeman.

Contemporary writers like my Facebook friends Robert F. Dorr and Rob Morris have been an inspiration, and these men have been my cheerleaders. I admire their ability to author multiple historical works. I also look forward with great anticipation to the HBO series *Masters of the Air*, created for television by Academy Award winners Steven Spielberg and Tom Hanks from the book *Masters of the Air: America's Bomber Boys Who Fought the Air War Against Nazi Germany* by the accomplished historian and educator Donald F. Miller.

Thanks to Colonel Robert Elliott, Irving Baum and Gregory Alexander of the 92nd Bomb Group Memorial Association for being an inspiration to me and for the priceless research its members have provided. In particular the published works and photo of the B-17 from the Bomb Group on the cover of this book.

Special Thanks to Anna Piro of Anna Piro Design of Wheaton, Illinois for her magnificent cover design . She captured my vison for that cover.

And Thank You to the staff at Authorhouse Publishing for their guidance and patience through this process.

Bibliography

Ambrose, Stephen E. *The Wild Blue: The Men and Boys Who Flew The B-24s Over Germany 1944–45*. New York: Simon & Shuster, 2001.

Astor, Gerald. *The Mighty Eighth- The Air War in Europe As Told By the Men Who Fought It.* New York: Dell, 1997

Bowman, Martin **W. B-17 Groups of the Eighth Air Force in Focus: A Photographic Album of the Eighth Air Force Groups That Went To War in The Boeing B-17 Flying Fortress.** Surrey, United Kingdom, Red Kite, 2004

Bowman, Martin W. B-**17 Flying Fortress Units of the Eighth Air Force (Part One)** Botley, Oxford, United Kingdom. Osprey Publishing., 2000

Brinkley, Douglas and Haskew, Martin. **The World War II Desk Reference.** New York, The Eisenhower Center for American Studies. Grand Central Press, A Division of Stonesong Press Inc. 2004

Dryjan, Joanne Paulinski **"From Heaven Into Hell.** Unpublished War Memories of Casimir Paulinski. Date Unknown.

Elliott, Robert D. Editor. **92nd Bomb Group (H) Fame's Favored Few**. Paducah, Turner Publishing 1996

Ethell, Jeffrey L/ **Bombers of WW II**. Ann Arbor:; Lowe & B. Hould, 2001

Freeman, Roger A, **The Mighty Eighth. A History of the Units, Men and Machines of the US 8th Air Force**; London, Cassell & Company, 1970.

Freeman, Roger A. **Mighty Eighth War Diary**. London, James Publishing 1981

Freeman, Roger A. **The Mighty Eighth in Color**, Stillwater, MN Specialty Press 1992

Nichol, John and Rennell, Tony. **The Last Escape: The Untold Story of Allied Prisoners of War in Europe 1944-45**, New York, Penguin Books; 2002

Sloan, John S. **The Route As Briefed: The History of the 92nd Bombardment Group USAAF 1943-1945/** Cleveland; Argus Press 1946

Videotaped Interviews with **Henry Roeber, Hubert O'Neill, George Sokolsky Kols, Arthur Pinzke and Royce McGillvary.**

WEBSITES

www.Geneology.com -A Property of Ancestry.com. Social Security Death Index

www.IMDB.com -Internet Movie Database

www.merkki.com -**World War II - Prisoners of War - Stalag Luft I, A collection of stories, photos, art and information on Stalag Luft 1**

www.Timesonline.com / Beaver County Times & Allegheny Times/Gino Piroli-Featured Columnist/ 6-21-2004, 6-26-2004, & 7-19-2004

www.B24.net

http://www.92ndma.org - 92nd USAAF-USAF Memorial Association

www.wwiimemorial.com/registry

http://www.abmc.gov/search American Battle Monuments Commission

http://phone.people.yahoo/com/PhoneSearch

www.mightyeighth.org/Historian

http://journalstar.com/lifestyles/announcements/obituaries/verlo-clayton/article

http://www.hempenfuneralhome.com/roeber,henry

http://findagrave.com

Standing in front to The Collings Foundation's "Nine 0 Nine"
Flying Fortress in Chicago, during its annual tour with a
B-24 Liberator. Mark flew as a passenger in this B-17.

About the Author

Mark Farina, a native Chicagoan, has worked as a sports announcer, photographer, sportswriter, and a government public relations specialist in a career spanning forty years. He is a respected sports public address announcer, having started as a fifteen-year-old sophomore at Steinmetz High School in 1975, and has announced high school championship games in baseball, football, basketball, wrestling, soccer, ice hockey, and girls rugby. He has been a P.A. Announcer for the Chicago Public Schools and for Chicago State University Cougars basketball, women's volleyball, and baseball. Farina attended Illinois State University as a Communications major, Columbia College Chicago as a Radio-TV major, and DePaul University. He has been an active member and officer in the Kiwanis International organization for over 25 years, and was a recipient of the" Lester Award" from Keep Chicago Beautiful with whom he served as a member of the Board of Directors. He has been happily married to Diane Paulinski Farina since 1993, they have a teenage son, Louis and a beautiful shepherd mix Bella.

Printed in the United States
By Bookmasters